Enjoy your book whenever and wherever you like!
WITH THIS BOOK YOU HAVE ALSO PURCHASED THE EBOOK EDITION

1. Go to www.campus.de/ebookinside.

2. To obtain your free ebook, please enter the following **download code** into the space below.

   »E-Book inside«:   GXMXN-ACFNC-78EGR

3. Select a **format** (MOBI/Kindle, EPUB or PDF).

4. Fill in the form with your email address and click the button at the end. You will then receive your **personal download link** via email.

T0136804

Integrated Intelligence

Ulrich Lichtenthaler is Professor of Management and Entrepreneurship at the International School of Management (ISM) in Cologne, Germany. He holds a Ph. D. degree in technology management and worked as a management consultant, successfully completing over 20 digital transformation, artificial intelligence and innovation projects over the past years. As an acknowledged expert, he is regularly booked as a keynote speaker, executive coach, and freelance consultant. He has taught executive education courses at leading business schools and has written multiple books and articles for journals and newspapers, such as *MIT Sloan Management Review* and *Wall Street Journal*.

Ulrich Lichtenthaler

Integrated Intelligence

Combining Human and Artificial Intelligence
for Competitive Advantage

Campus Verlag
Frankfurt/New York

ISBN 978-3-593-51203-7 Print
ISBN 978-3-593-44392-8 E-Book (PDF)
ISBN 978-3-593-44393-5 E-Book (PDF)

Coverdesign: total italic, Thierry Wijnberg, Amsterdam/Berlin
Typesetting: Publikations Atelier, Dreieich
Fonts: Sabon Next and DIN
Printing: Beltz Grafische Betriebe GmbH, Bad Langensalza
Printed in Germany

www.campus.de

Contents

Preface

How can businesses profit from artificial intelligence? The book addresses this key strategic question by examining the possibilities for gaining and sustaining a competitive advantage in an intelligence-based competitive environment. As such, it goes considerably beyond viewing AI applications as isolated tools that may enhance the efficiency of established business processes. Rather, it considers the interplays of artificial and human intelligence that enable firms to develop completely new products, services, processes, and business models. Besides many opportunities, the growing importance of AI also brings major threats for the traditional business of companies and for the jobs of some employees. In addition, the recent advances in different fields of AI have led to the emergence of major ethical questions, whose importance cannot be overestimated. In this exciting and challenging context, this book focuses on the strategic and competitive rather than ethical implications of AI.

This book is aimed at managers and executives, and it does not require prior knowledge in information technology or engineering. Instead, it shows how firms may thrive in a digital future by achieving an intelligence-based competitive advantage. As such, the book is targeted at practitioners rather than researchers. Nonetheless, some concepts, such as the intelligence-based view of business performance, may also provide a contribution to management research. In fact, many parts of the book have been adapted from some of my previous journal articles, which 'survived' review processes before publication and which also include a more detailed literature overview. However, the focus of this book is on managerial implications. Therefore, it deemphasizes discussions of the academic literature. For a more detailed literature review, please consult the published journal articles, to which I refer in several chapters.

The book offers some guidance and support to practitioners in the exciting journey towards intelligence-based future competition. My previous consulting expertise and ongoing collaborations with companies suggest that some of the insights of the book actually provide helpful starting points for managers. If readers are most interested in the relevance of AI and the situation at other companies, part A may be particularly interesting. If the focus is more on implementation challenges, part E and especially the I3 – Integrated Intelligence Incubator are worth reading. At the end of chapter 14 you will find an overview of the major characteristics of Integrated Intelligence. HR professionals may be particularly interested in part D and the beginning of part E, which address the role of employee attitudes, new leadership styles, and the future role of the HR department. For academics, part B with the conceptual framework for an intelligence-based view may be relevant. Overall, the largest part of the impact of AI is yet to come. I wish you best of luck with your AI initiatives and look forward to receiving your feedback and hopefully meeting you at some future event. Please do not hesitate to contact me: www.integratedintelligence.de

Cologne, February 2020
Prof. Dr. Ulrich Lichtenthaler

Part A

Relevance

 **Chapter 1**

The competitive relevance of artificial intelligence

Can your business successfully compete without using artificial intelligence (AI) in the future? No. Can your company successfully compete without human expertise and human intelligence (HI) in the future? No. So far, these questions are no-brainers. But do you think that your company takes the necessary steps to benefit from AI and HI in the future? Well ... honestly no. If these could be your own answers, you are quite representative for many companies at present. These are very typical responses that you will get from the executives and managers in many established companies when asking some quick questions about the relevance of AI. Many companies have acknowledged the relevance of AI. Beyond merely realizing the importance, many of them actively utilize AI, and this is true for large companies as well as small and medium-sized enterprises across a large variety of different sectors, including product-based as well as service-driven industries. Thus, is everything fine with the competitiveness of those established companies in an intelligence-based future? Most unfortunately, the answer again is ... no.

Many companies have accepted the growing importance of AI in terms of advanced data analytics and intelligent algorithms. You can hardly avoid regular news updates about the latest developments and accomplishments of AI in the news, press, social media, and many other channels. Despite the clear understanding of both AI and human expertise being essential in the future, however, most companies do not act accordingly. If you answer 'no' to the question of whether your firm takes the necessary steps for profiting from AI and HI, this is a strong initial signal that your organization may be in trouble, at least in the medium to long run. However, your insight is an important first step towards strategic transformation. Paradoxically, the situation is often even more difficult at companies where executives are fully convinced that they are on the right path with regard to AI. These companies have usually started some strategic initiatives towards implementing selected smart algorithms and the latest technology for data analytics, but most of these companies only claim to be well-prepared for intelligence-based competition.

In fact, these companies only seem to be well-prepared at first glance. When you take a closer look, the leading position of these companies is only a superficial perception, and this wrong perception may be dangerous. So do you personally take the necessary steps to benefit from AI and HI in your everyday business activities? Maybe yes … and maybe you have initiated some fascinating strategic initiatives for implementing AI, which work well and which are quite successful from an operational and financial perspective. These success stories may be important, and they may constitute major steps towards proficiently competing in the future. Nonetheless, you most likely are not among the very small minority of companies that are in fact leading the intelligence revolution. Rather, the likelihood is over 90 percent that you and your company have a wrong perception of being well prepared for the digital future – at least to some degree. So what is the situation with regard to AI in the vast majority of companies, really?

Many firms from a variety of sectors – such as automotive, chemicals, electronics, machinery, and pharmaceuticals – are reluctant to fully leverage the benefits of AI, willingly or unwillingly. Even those companies that are actively pursuing strategic AI initiatives usually focus on replacing some human work by AI in selected business processes. However, merely using AI to substitute for human work will usually be insufficient. This logic of replacing humans may be an important first step in using AI. In many situations, it may be implemented quite easily because the underlying business processes do not change. Therefore, it is indeed a good start for leveraging AI. Nonetheless, it is only a suitable first step and nothing more. In particular, replacing human work typically helps companies to enhance their efficiency. The cost savings that are associated with this substitution are a natural next step in the automation of business activities. However, these smart automation processes will become standard procedures in the future. Consequently, a company's competitors will also master these AI applications, whose competitive benefits will fall short of most executives' expectations.

This is not to say that the efficiency gains from AI are not relevant with regard to a firm's financial performance. The optimization processes may very well have important financial consequences. However, they will not enable companies to gain and to sustain an intelligence-based competitive advantage in the future. In this respect, companies rather need to integrate their AI applications with specific human expertise. While it may be challenging for competitors to imitate particular human competencies, it will be even more challenging to copy specific combinations of human and artificial intelligence. This is what integrated intelligence is all about. It focuses on the interfaces of human and artificial intelligence. For many isolated applications of AI, standardized solutions are being developed at the moment. A large part of these solutions will be quite interchangeable and will further be commoditized over time. Therefore, they do not constitute a suitable basis for a sustainable competitive advantage.

Rather, the consequences of the evolution towards AI will substantially exceed an isolated use of AI. Instead, companies will significantly alter their entire intelligence architecture, which affects key business processes, established organizational designs, and typical forms of collaboration. In this regard, AI will also have a major impact on humans' everyday activities. Consequently, businesses need to actively manage multiple types of intelligence, including AI, HI as well as a meta-intelligence for transforming their human and artificial intelligence in line with their long-term strategies and dominant managerial approaches. Thus, businesses need Intelligence^x – encompassing various types of AI and HI as well as meta-intelligence. Along with the combination of AI and HI, the dynamic transformation and renewal of a company's intelligence architecture provides the basis for achieving an intelligence-based competitive advantage that may be sustained over longer or even unlimited periods. Only those companies that are aiming at a sustainable competitive advantage are well-prepared for future competition. The vast majority of businesses, in contrast, neglect developing integrated intelligence, and they only have a wrong perception of being well prepared for intelligence-based competition.

AI has come a long way

The application of AI is more ubiquitous than you may believe. What was your last touchpoint with AI? Most probably, you do not remember it. Most certainly, it was today. Nonetheless, you do not remember it because you did not recognize it. AI is everywhere around us, making our lives easier – or at least parts of our lives. We hardly notice it because companies integrate it so seamlessly in software applications, hardware devices, and many processes that we already take for granted. Examples are auto corrections by your smartphone, which improve over time because the algorithm learns which words you want to use. Another smartphone application of AI are face recognition technologies. Beyond mere smartphone applications, many people regularly interact with customer service bots that are based on AI. You may also think of Google's Duplex solution, which integrates several AI technologies to enable an AI assistant to make calls with a close-to-human voice.

Beyond these applications for customers, AI transforms the production processes, data handling and channel management of companies. Moreover, self-driving cars are only one well-known solution among many more fascinating applications of AI. In light of the growing proficiency of AI applications, many people now fear that AI at some point may replace their own jobs. Yes, AI will create new jobs, but it will also replace human work. Still, AI's impact on human work remains controversial. This is largely due to the fact that we have only seen the beginning, the application of AI so far being limited relative to its potential. Therefore, the competitive effect is already noticeable, but the largest part of the impact is still to come. Sometimes, it is surprising to what degree many small and medium-sized companies have already adopted particular AI applications that you would rather have expected to see in dedicated departments of large multinational companies. Despite the surprisingly broad use of AI, however, the focus of most companies is on a few selected applications.

In this regard, AI may be considered a logical strategic move in an evolutionary process that started at least several decades ago.[1] AI has come a long way, and it is not a trend that only started a few years ago. In fact, the roots of AI are often traced back to 1956, when the term 'Artificial Intelligence' was coined for the two-month Dartmouth Summer Research Project. The project proposal included ambitious goals for the short research period, and some of these goals have not been fully achieved today despite the significant advances of AI. Beyond the term AI, we can even go further back in time referring to 1679 when Gottfried Wilhelm Leibniz developed the binary number system, following an example set in ancient China. In 1936, Alan Turing proposed the concept for the Turing machine, which provided an important foundation for computer technology.

On this basis, the 1960s and 1970s brought the first wave of IT impact in Western companies. Here, the focus of IT primarily was on automating relatively isolated activities in the value chain. During this time, Intel also developed the first commercially available microprocessor. The second wave of IT impact occurred during the 1980s and 1990s. The particular strategic emphasis during this time was enabling coordination and integration across multiple different activities. During this period, in 1989, the World Wide Web was invented by the English scientist Tim Berners-Lee. In 1997, IBM's Deep Blue defeated Garry Kasparov at chess. Subsequently, in 1999, the British entrepreneur Kevin Ashton proposed the term 'Internet of Things'. We now experience the third wave of IT impact in companies, roughly since the year 2000. In 2012, Apple introduced the intelligent personal assistant Siri. By means of sensors, big data, and smart algorithms, products increasingly feature computer components to enable all parts to network with all other parts.

With particular emphasis on production processes, AI is a next step in the evolution that started with 'industry 1.0' in terms of using steam power for production based on James Watt's patent for a steam engine in 1781. Typically, 1913 is considered as the start of mass production and 'industry 2.0' because Henry Ford manufactured the Model T on an assembly line. With a growing use of computer technology in production processes, the next step in terms of 'industry 3.0' included the IT-based automation of manufacturing activities. Today, we experience 'industry 4.0', which focuses on digital connectivity and AI. The terms digitization, digitalization, and digital transformation have been increasingly used since 2010, and the following years also led to an explosion in the use of the term artificial intelligence. With regard to production processes, companies increasingly use AI to leverage the data that they started to collect with the digitalization of their manufacturing processes in the previous years.

From a strategic perspective, it is essential to view AI as a next wave of IT impact in business activities and as a logical further step of automating production processes. Here, it is particularly important to acknowledge the dynamic understanding of the scope of AI. Some advanced applications were regarded as AI in previous times, but they are largely considered standard routines today. Thus, the understanding of AI substantially develops over time, and it now includes the latest technology in the fields of advanced data analytics and intelligent algorithms. In some years, today's most advanced applications will be considered relatively standard procedures, which are mastered by the majority of companies, thus limiting the potential to achieve a competitive advantage on that basis. For example, you may think about the robot-based automation of production processes in the automotive industry, which started several decades ago. Partly, this automation was considered AI in the past, but it is merely standard routine now due to the dynamic understanding of the scope of AI.[2]

Why are we experiencing such hype about AI just right now? This is an excellent question if we consider the long evolution of AI until today. Of course, this evolution has not occurred continuously. Instead, there have been periods of major advances, which were followed by periods of limited further developments, leading to a reduction of funding in the development of AI. These periods are typically termed 'AI winters', and we witnessed several of them over the past decades. In contrast, there is a huge hype about AI right now. In fact, Gartner put two key fields of AI, machine learning and deep learning, at the top of its hype cycle analysis in 2018. Some other fields, such as artificial general intelligence and deep reinforcement learning, are still far from reaching this inflection point. With regard to machine learning and deep learning, however, we may have reached a peak of somewhat inflated expectations with regard to their potential opportunities. Thus, there may be some disillusionment over the next years until a sustainable level of productivity based on these key fields of AI will have been achieved.

Nonetheless, there are good reasons why the competitive impact of AI will continue beyond the hype that we experience at present. There have been major improvements in various technology fields in recent years, which jointly drive the business impact of AI. Examples are advanced analytics and voice recognition, which may be leveraged by means of enhanced connectivity and cloud solutions. These developments help to exploit the technological infrastructure and pools of big data which are increasingly collected due to the growing digitalization of business processes. Thus, the danger of experiencing yet another 'AI winter' is relatively limited in the next years. While the hype cycle may have reached the inflection point at least for some of the key fields of AI, the vast part of the competitive impact of AI is yet to come. Without a stronger use of AI, most companies' investments in digital transformation would not pay off because firms will be unable to leverage all the data that they collect as a part of their digitalization initiatives exclusively based on human work.

With the most substantial business changes of AI still ahead, it is particularly important to examine the strategic implications for your firm right now. It is key to adopt a strategic perspective, which examines the impact of AI on your business in the medium to long run. There is no alternative to developing a thorough understanding of the changes for your industry, for your business model, and for competitive advantage. There are some excellent previous publications of the impact of AI. For example, Ajay Agrawal, Joshua Gans, and Avi Goldfarb describe the economics of AI in their 2018 book entitled *Prediction Machines*. In addition, Paul R. Daugherty and H. James Wilson discuss the implications of AI for the human-machine interface in their 2018 book entitled *Human + Machine*. If we take for granted the underlying economic logic of AI and the need for a closer collaboration of humans and machines, executives still face the challenge of developing appropriate proactive and reactive strategic initiatives to stay ahead of competition in an intelligence-based future business arena. Here, many key questions from a strategic and competitive point of view remain open in most companies.

There is a long road ahead

AI has come a long way so far, but for most companies the largest part of the AI transformation is still ahead. In this regard, there is no need for viewing the growing use of AI primarily as a threat to a company's established competitive position. For most companies, there are just as many opportunities as there are threats due to AI. In particular, understanding AI as a next step in a long evolution of business activities towards automation and IT helps to get a more realistic perspective on the potential benefits and risks of AI. Yes, there are severe challenges ahead. However, just doing nothing is not an option in light of the fundamental nature of the transformations. Many AI applications are quite complex from a technology point of view. What is even more critical for executives and general managers, however, is the impact on their firms' business models and business processes. General managers do not have to become experts in the underlying technologies. Instead, it will be the application of the solutions and their impact on the established businesses and competitors which will separate winners from losers.

Above all, there will be major shifts with regard to the value chain and the business ecosystems of many companies. Executives need to acknowledge that many of these shifts cannot fully be foreseen today. Thus, some level of experimentation and simultaneously pursuing multiple strategic options will be inevitable. Nonetheless, there is no immediate need to be nervous immediately and to embark on a course of aimless activism. At the same time, however, wait-and-see is not a suitable strategic option either. Instead, it is key to thoroughly examine the strategic effects of AI and their interplays with HI on the particular situation of your company. Here, specific attention needs to be paid to the dynamics of competition with regard to new activities in the value chain, such as data analytics, and new stakeholders in the ecosystem, such as IT service providers. Without developing a detailed analytical picture of the future competitive environment, most AI initiatives will remain isolated solutions in response to minor opportunities and threats. These solutions may have important positive effects, but they usually will not be sufficient for answering the key strategic questions for an intelligence-based competitive future.

When you try to make sense of the impact of AI on your business, it is helpful to separate different concepts and consequences as much as possible to clear a path through the forest of AI and digitalization. The contested definition, unclear terminology, and vague understanding have contributed to the perceived complexity of the topic, and they have already blocked the implementation of many AI initiatives at the idea stage – although the initiatives appeared to be quite promising from a conceptual point of view. In this respect, it is often useful to structure relevant trends with regard to three major categories: technology enablers, market applications, and management challenges.[3] This systematization draws on the well-established categorization of technology push vs. market pull effects with management challenges in-between because they may result from balancing both types of influences. Besides moving some of the specific discussion of AI to the more familiar arena of managing innovation and change, this systematization helps companies to select and organize for a suitable strategic response to the variety of trends that are associated with AI and digitalization.

First, concerning technology enablers, recent advances in AI and related technology fields provide the basis for the new strategic opportunities and threats that arise. More specifically, the technology enablers range from hardware solutions to software applications with some cross-fertilization of the improvements in hardware and software. With regard to hardware, some relevant enablers of the growing use of AI may be found in robotics, 3D printing, embedded sensors, and further customized hardware. With respect to software, efficient data storage solutions and cloud applications along with enhanced data security technologies enable new AI applications. New connectivity solutions help to leverage and to connect the advances in hardware and software, which further provide the basis for new interfaces and interplays of AI and human expertise. For example, many products are considered 'smart' because they include some kind of sensor. However, it is not the sensor per se that enables a product to become 'smart'. Rather, it is the connectivity component that helps to transfer some data to or from the sensor that enables 'intelligent' products. Often, these technology enablers are considered the core of the AI revolution. While this is partly correct, the technological factors are only enablers. The revolution comes from changes in the business logic due to fully exploiting the new technologies in the markets.

Second, regarding market applications, the benefits of AI derive from a large variety of applications across different sectors. Some of these market applications are primarily directed at enhancing the efficiency of established solutions. Some other applications are targeted at offering radical innovations by providing completely new solutions. On this basis, there is also a varying degree of interaction between AI solutions and human work. With regard to efficiency benefits, AI helps to optimize production and many other processes. This includes smart grid applications in the energy sector as well as intelligent logistics, digital banking, and digital insurance applications, which often focus on optimization and efficiency gains. In contrast, more innovation-driven use cases of AI comprise autonomous driving, smart homes, digital entertainment, and smart healthcare. Some applications allow for innovation and efficiency benefits at the same time. For instance, credit card companies rely on AI for fraud detection. There are innovative solutions for making credit cards more secure while simultaneously reducing the costs of fraud management.

Third, the interplay of technology enablers and market applications of AI leads to major management challenges. These management challenges involve strategic topics at a conceptual level as well as operational topics, which focus strongly on the implementation of AI. At a strategic level, executives need to address AI and its link to human expertise, for example in strategic planning and product development. Moreover, the effects of AI on the established managerial logic in a given industry need to be taken into account. Here, AI's effects on a company's business model in terms of value proposition, value creation, and value capture deserve particular attention along with potential changes in the customer experiences and customer relationship management. More operational aspects often focus on value chain topics and include back-end processes and autonomous analytics to enable a smooth application of AI. The strategic and operational topics lead to the specific organizational challenges of AI. In particular, people-related topics play a key role here, such as talent management and leadership development. Moreover, collaboration-related topics, such as cross-functional teams and a growing agility of processes with innovation sprints, call for revising a firm's established management procedures and practices.

The majority of challenges that executives face with respect to AI and the transformation of their company's intelligence derive from a combination of technology push as well as market pull effects. Nonetheless, it is helpful to conceptually separate technology enablers, market applications, and management challenges because usually there is a focus on technology push or market pull. This particular focus on either technology push or market pull leads to different managerial challenges and to a different procedure of implementing AI initiatives. In the case of technology push, for instance, there may be a new algorithm for enhancing machine efficiency. As a consequence, a firm may start a strategic planning process, which will finally lead to implementing an AI for controlling the use of power and other resources in the manufacturing process, leading to a better price/performance ratio for the firm's customers. In the case of market pull, for example, customers may expect higher service levels than a company is able to provide with its existing customer care team. In response, the company revises its internal organization to include customer service bots, which can automatically handle a large portion of customer service inquiries.

By disentangling technology enablers, market applications, and management challenges, executives can proactively and reactively respond to the AI revolution in a more systematic way. In addition, it facilitates the targeted utilization of a company's established planning processes, resource allocation procedures, and key performance indicators. This link between firms' established business activities and new AI applications is particularly critical when they move beyond relatively isolated applications of AI. To achieve a competitive advantage in the future, it will be insufficient to merely view AI as some type of IT tool that primarily leads to technological changes. Instead, the growing need for integrated intelligence – comprising AI, HI, and a meta-intelligence – will inevitably lead to a high relevance and strong interdependency of multiple technology enablers, market applications, and management challenges.

Acknowledging this strategic complexity and developing a systematic approach is an essential first step towards achieving a competitive advantage in the future. To prepare for this future, the growing competitive relevance of AI cannot be ignored – and should not be ignored. It will be a long way until the competitive impact of AI will fully unfold in most industries because what we have observed in the past years has only been the beginning. Most importantly, the core strategic impact will derive from integrated intelligence and from the interplay of AI with HI rather than from the pure implementation of AI. In this respect, most companies across a large variety of industries have not undertaken any significant managerial action. One key issue in this regard would be to move beyond applying AI for enhancing efficiency in order to stimulate innovation and growth. Here, key insights may be gained from the next chapters by analyzing your company's position and comparing it with the world's most innovative companies.

 Chapter 2

The isolated ignorance of many established businesses

The competitive relevance of AI will further grow over the next years. Thus, executives should not ignore the competitive impact of AI. However, many businesses do exactly that – they largely neglect the opportunities and threats of AI. Rather than ignoring the growing possibilities of AI, executives need to examine the opportunities and threats in a balanced way. While ignoring AI does not help, a state of shock is also inappropriate. Indeed, AI has some specific characteristics which will lead to major transformations. In essence, however, it is yet another disruptive technological evolution. Many companies have a strong history of successfully embedding new technologies in their established business processes. These firms can actually be proud of their historical trajectories in response to technological changes. Above all, these companies have accumulated substantial experience and learning effects in transforming their organizations.

This historical evolution may be turned into an advantage for established companies – under the condition that it is used wisely for initiating appropriate strategic responses. While taking the recent advances in AI seriously, companies should address them with some level of self-confidence. If appropriate strategic measures are undertaken, AI will offer just as many opportunities as threats. Consequently, the question comes up how important AI is, really – not in terms of ideal strategic planning and conceptual analysis, but in terms of implemented initiatives and operational action in firms from different sectors. How do executives and companies react to the new possibilities that are associated with AI? What is the typical strategic response of firms from various industries? What can we learn from the most innovative companies? How do these leading companies respond to the recent developments in AI? And finally, how does your company score with regard to using AI?

How do firms respond to recent advances in AI?

The strategic relevance of AI is relatively well accepted in many medium-sized and large companies by now. The vast media attention concerning the recent advances in AI has ensured that the new possibilities have not gone unnoticed by most companies. However, acknowledging the strategic relevance is merely a first step. In contrast to a relatively broad agreement on the competitive relevance of AI, the strategic priority that is placed on this topic differs substantially among companies. In fact, many firms have acknowledged the general strategic relevance of AI, but it is not – or at least not yet – on the top of their agendas. Even if AI is considered a strategic priority, this does not necessarily lead to operational action with regard to implementing AI programs and initiatives. Some companies regard AI as a strategic priority, but have not yet taken any particular action. Accordingly, we may distinguish five groups of companies, depending on the degree of strategic priority and the degree of operational action that is taken with regard to AI (Figure 1).

The first group is a relatively large number of businesses that are characterized by limited strategic priority and limited operational action with regard to AI. Accordingly, these companies may be considered as 'Observers' because they have not yet acknowledged the strategic relevance of AI or do not regard AI as a strategic priority. Consequently, they primarily observe what happens. The executives of many of these companies agree that AI will be relevant in their firms at least at some point in the future. So far, however, they have placed other initiatives and projects at the top of their agendas because they appear to be more critical in the short term. Thus, AI may become a strategic priority in these companies in the future, but up to now it is not a top priority. In addition, these companies have

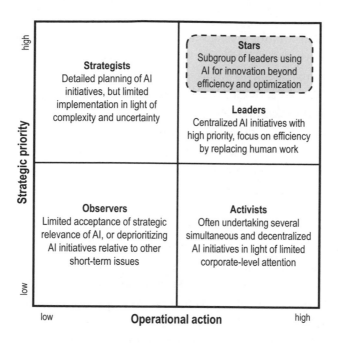

Figure 1: Strategic relevance of AI in different groups of businesses

not started any particular activities or programs to explore or to exploit AI solutions. Rather, these businesses are in a 'wait and see' position. While some of them are completely inactive, some at least try to develop a thorough understanding of the particular impact of AI on their organizations. Thus, only a subset of these companies is fully ignorant with regard to AI. The others largely neglect AI because they have not made it a strategic priority and they have not started managerial action.

The second group of businesses is a noteworthy set of organizations that place limited strategic priority on AI. Nonetheless, these companies undertake at least some operational action with regard to AI. Therefore, this group of companies is termed 'Activists' because they have started some AI initiatives although the topic does not enjoy high strategic priority. In light of the limited top executive attention, there are often decentralized AI activities in different business units and departments. Often, there are several simultaneous projects, but a masterplan for coordinating these activities and for leveraging potential synergies is missing. In some of these firms, the AI activities have been started with the formal consent of top management, whereas in some other companies the responsibility for the AI activities is fully decentralized. However, all of the AI activities of these companies are relatively isolated. Thus, potential interdependencies among different initiatives are not leveraged, and this tendency may still be considered as some isolated ignorance. Consequently, there are usually major opportunities for further enhancing the AI activities in these companies based on a systematic, focused, and collaborative organizational approach.

In contrast to the second group of companies, the third group is characterized by a high strategic importance of AI combined with limited operational action. These companies are called 'Strategists' because they see the need for addressing AI, but most of them struggle with regard to choosing suitable implementation steps. Some of these companies have relatively detailed procedures for monitoring the advances of AI technology in order to be well prepared if they take the decision to actually implement some AI applications. In light of the complexity of many AI applications and the changes that are needed for fully leveraging these applications, however, the firms in this group are reluctant to take bold steps towards implementation. They realize that developing a perfect solution will hardly be possible in the first step. Rather than viewing the need for experimentation as an opportunity, however, the environmental uncertainty and risk that are often associated with AI block the implementation of AI initiatives in these companies. The executives usually believe that a well-informed decision to put potential AI initiatives on 'hold' is more suitable at present than investing in fields with an uncertain payback. Time will tell whether this hesitant approach is successful.

The fourth group of companies combines a high strategic priority of AI with specific operational action. Therefore, these companies are termed 'Leaders'. They typically pursue some AI activities which are centrally coordinated at corporate level and which are pursued with high priority. While some of these companies undertake large and relatively broad AI programs, others pursue more focused and relatively lean AI initiatives. Whatever the scope of the AI activities, they are systematically managed and executed. With regard to the strategic direction of the AI initiatives, there are substantial differences among the firms in this group. Most of the companies that are part of the 'Leaders' focus on using AI for increasing the efficiency of established processes and business models. Consequently, they primarily implement AI solutions to replace human work in order to achieve some benefits in terms of optimization and cost reduction. Accordingly, the strategic intent of the AI initiatives is relatively narrow and focused on improving established operations, processes, and business activities. The center of attention is the advanced automation of processes that could not be automated without advanced algorithms and data analytics in the past.

The strategic direction of the AI activities in these companies is relatively limited because the full potential of using AI is largely neglected. In particular, the 'Leaders' often leave the potential of AI for innovation and growth unconsidered. As such, even companies that believe being on a good way with regard to AI do not fully explore the strategic opportunities of AI, let alone exploit the full business potential. In particular, most of the 'Leaders' do not sufficiently consider the interdependencies between AI and human expertise. Instead, these companies largely focus on substituting human work by means of AI. This focus enables efficiency gains and temporary competitive advantages. In the medium to long term, however, the competitive impact of these AI activities will be relatively limited. Many companies in this group are regarded as good examples for successfully implementing AI by competitors and other firms. While this is correct to some degree, it is only part of the truth.

The companies in this group have one major strategic focus in their AI implementation, i.e. increasing efficiency by replacing human work. The successful implementation of these activities ensures that the AI initiatives are successful from a financial perspective. Moreover, this financial success is encouraging, and it typically leads to a self-reinforcing cycle of extending the AI applications to achieve further optimization benefits. At the same time, the success of these companies limits their strategic intent to systematically pursue a different dimension of AI beyond efficiency programs. Consequently, they do not systematically address AI for achieving innovation and growth by developing completely new solutions, services, and business models which would transform their established operations. While the uncertainty and risk of these activities may be higher, the strategic impact and potential competitive advantage may also be higher in the long run. Nonetheless, most 'Leaders' do not actively address this promising dimension of AI applications.

Thus, it is inappropriate to consider all companies that are strategically pursing efficiency-driven AI activities as shining examples. A thorough evaluation is somewhat more complex. There is a subgroup of companies among the 'Leaders' that systematically uses AI for innovation and growth beyond efficiency and optimization. These companies do not neglect efficiency benefits, but they balance their efficiency-centered activities on the one hand with creating new markets based on radically novel solutions on the other. In the new markets, they may gain monopoly rents for a certain time. Subsequently, they may still enjoy a competitive advantage because it is harder for competitors to imitate completely novel solutions. Accordingly, only those companies with a balanced approach can be considered 'Stars'. They are a subset of the 'Leaders', and their success in strengthening efficiency does not lead to complacency, but it rather is a driver of exploring further ways to leverage AI for completely new purposes. Thus, they pursue a more comprehensive and balanced approach towards profiting from AI than the remaining 'Leaders' and the companies in the other groups.

How does the historical evolution matter?

Those companies that have acknowledged the strategic relevance and that have undertaken operational action with regard to AI are better prepared for the growing competitive relevance of AI than most other firms. Even for the companies that are currently lagging behind, however, it is usually not too late to benefit from the opportunities of AI while avoiding the potential threats. Viewing AI as a next step in the automation of business processes is typically a helpful perspective because it enables companies to categorize the move towards AI in the context of previous technological changes that they successfully mastered in the past. As such, it helps firms to acknowledge the game-changing nature of AI while simultaneously entering this new competitive arena with some level of confidence because of previous successes in the history of their firms. At present, it may be quite late to start systematic AI initiatives, depending on the particular sector and type of business. In most cases, however, it is not yet too late.

By taking some bold strategic moves, many companies can quickly catch up with their current and potential competitors. In addition, they might even leapfrog some other companies, which only focus on enhancing their established business processes and business models by means of AI. While those companies may forego many of the opportunities, other firms that have a late start can bypass them by developing completely new solutions for their customers while not ignoring the potential efficiency gains from AI. Thus, the window of opportunity for profiting from AI is relatively wide open for most firms, and it will still be open for some time. However, this opportunity period is not unlimited, and the time to act is now. While it is not too late yet, there is also no time for further inactivity. Executives may often build on their firms' particular human expertise and prior experiences in managing technological change. Thus, they may leverage their company's history of successful transformation and change. Nonetheless, it would be entirely wrong to downplay the potential impact of AI based on an excessive confidence and hubris due to a strong competitive position at present.

In particular, it is time to fully grasp the potential competitive impact of AI over the next years. In many industries, AI will have a disruptive impact. As such, it does not only enable radical innovations with a high degree of novelty. Instead, it allows for disrupting established industries with respect to their traditional products, services, and solutions. In this regard, AI-based solutions may not immediately be relevant to the entire market. Over time, however, the AI-enabled segment of the market will increase, leading to the disruption of many companies' established business models.[1] This expected trajectory of multiple sectors underscores that the competitive relevance of AI goes far beyond optimization and efficiency gains. Usually, these disruptions do not occur within a few months. Consequently, companies that may have a late start can still catch up, but the window of opportunity will close in the foreseeable future. If a company does not actively participate in the disruption of its industry, other players will do so – with the potential for substantial negative effects on a company's business, including bankruptcy. Thus, it is the disruptive nature rather than the radical novelty of AI solutions that leads to their significant opportunities and threats.

A key factor for these disruptive effects does not boil down to the intelligent algorithms or smart components that AI enables. The disruption does not derive from the products, services, or solutions per se. Rather, it often depends on the new business models that AI facilitates. Installing additional sensors in established products helps companies to collect data at large scales. On this basis, intelligent algorithms enable advanced analytics of the big data. These largely product-driven changes would still allow for remaining successful by continuing with many traditional behaviors. However, a new business model, such as predictive maintenance based on AI or offering machines as a service, turn the technological advances into a disruptive evolution, which changes the competitive rules of the game. To arrive at these fundamental changes, it is typically not enough merely to focus on AI. Instead, executives need to consider AI as a basis for a broader set of changes with particular emphasis on business model innovation. If a company is not willing to move into this direction, other players will be open to take these steps. Accordingly, executives need to carefully observe and forecast the competitive interplay of multiple innovations.

In this regard, many companies can build on corporate foresight and technology intelligence processes, which they have established in the past in order to stay ahead of relevant trends and business transformations. These processes are partly conducted by dedicated units for trend analyses and technology foresight, especially in large firms, and they have proved helpful in coping with many technological trends over the past decades. In the case of AI, however, they will only be helpful if they do not blind companies with regard to the disruptive changes and business model transformations. In many situations, the competitive impact of these non-technological innovations will be much more severe than the pure effect of the advanced data analytics and intelligent algorithms alone. Accordingly, it will be insufficient to praise successful technological evolutions of a company in the past and to point out that the technological consequences per se may be relatively limited, which is actually true for several fields of AI. The move towards new business models, particularly AI-enabled digital platforms, may turn a historically stable industry upside down although the technological novelty of the underlying AI solutions may be quite limited.

Finally, a specific feature of many new business models that are enabled by AI may complicate a suitable strategic response. In this regard, a firm's historical evolution may also be a double-edged sword, which may benefit or limit a company's opportunities to profit from AI. The implementation of AI often has exponential effects, which may take various forms. With regard to revenues, for example, AI may enable a service business to capture only a few dollars or even cents for a single new service transaction. However, the number of service transactions may grow exponentially at least for some time, for example based on a platform model. In the end, the multitude of small transactions leads to a multi-billion dollar business. On a different note, exponential effects can also occur with regard to the costs of business activities. A simple app or digital assistant may perform tasks that still required extensive human interaction a few years ago. These exponential effects accelerate the disruption of industries based on new business models at least for a limited period. If established companies systematically consider and adapt this exponential thinking, they are often well positioned to leverage their history of successful innovation and transformation. However, if executives do not take into account these particular competitive effects of AI and related evolutions, a decline of their firm's competitive position is likely to start and to speed up in the years to come. In this regard, it is essential to develop a detailed understanding of the impact of AI and digitalization on your firm.

How does your company score?

How would you rank your company with regard to the strategic priority and operational action of AI initiatives? It is relatively easy to sketch some general criteria for these two dimensions. Concerning strategic priority, you may assess some of the following questions. Has your business set up an AI initiative based on a formal decision of the top management team? Has your firm developed a corporate-level AI strategy? Are discussions of AI activities regularly part of executive meetings? Are AI activities part of the company's planning and budgeting processes? Do you have a company-wide coordination of AI activities? Have some communities-of-practice emerged for AI activities in your firm? Regarding operational action, you may examine some of the following questions. Has your firm implemented any AI solutions? Does your firm have an AI initiative that actually proceeds rather than being regularly put on hold in light of other projects? Does the AI team receive sufficient support from other departments and business units? Does the AI team have sufficient funding for proficiently undertaking its activities? Does top management attempt to speed up the AI initiative? Answering 'yes' to these questions indicates a relatively high level of strategic priority and operational action, respectively.

An assessment of these two dimensions may be easily formalized in a checklist. However, more important than a general benchmarking of your company relative to all types of companies is comparing your firm with others in a similar context. For example, the size of a company in terms of revenues and employees has a major impact on the strategic management of AI initiatives. In addition, the industry where a firm is active, usually has a strong impact on the strategic priority and operational action with regard to AI. Beyond that, the strategic focus and intent of a company's AI activities differ strongly across firms from the automotive, electronics, financial services, healthcare, and machinery sectors. However, a company should not only compare its activities with the 'usual suspects', for example its established competitors. A particular feature of AI applications in the broader context of digital transformation is the decreasing importance of industry boundaries. Thus, companies may start offering platforms or integrated services based on AI which constitute significant new competition to firms in completely different sectors. Accordingly, it would be insufficient to merely consider a company's position in AI relative to its established competitors.

Instead, a company's position concerning the strategic relevance and operational action with regard to AI fundamentally depends on the individual strategic decision of the top management team. It is often surprising to see relatively small companies from sectors with a limited emphasis on innovation undertaking major AI initiatives because the executives perceive a strong need or benefit from bold strategic moves towards implementing AI. While some firms are relatively open to proactively pursuing the transformation of their intelligence architecture towards a stronger focus on AI, many others are reluctant to do so based on strategic decisions and corporate cultures that are not conducive to major organizational changes. While the opportunities and threats of AI are not equal for all companies, AI will have an effect on most firms' business activities at least in the medium to long term. By asking yourself some of the questions above to assess the strategic priority and operational action for AI, you immediately get a detailed understanding of your company's position and of potential ways for strengthening the AI activities. In this regard, it may be particularly insightful to examine the activities of the leading innovators worldwide.

Chapter 3

The strategic focus of the world's most innovative companies

When you think about the world's leading companies in AI, you might think of Google, IBM, Microsoft and some other technology companies. In light of the discussion in the previous chapter about the particular benefits of using AI for innovation rather than exclusively for enhancing efficiency, there may be a lot to learn from the world's most innovative companies. These companies are most successful in profiting from new technologies and solutions. In particular, they are well known for successfully developing new markets based on new technologies and solutions. This focus on innovation is the key difference between companies that are considered 'Leaders' in the field of AI and the subset of 'Stars' among the leading firms. The 'Leaders' and 'Stars' are both proficient in optimizing their existing processes and activities by means of AI. However, only the 'Stars' are able to leverage AI for transforming their businesses and for developing new markets, in which they will likely achieve a leading competitive position. In fact, innovation is a major determinant of corporate performance, and superior innovation can enable a sustainable competitive advantage.[1]

From an academic perspective, many different studies have shown positive performance effects of systematic innovation, and recent reviews and meta-analyses further underscore the importance of innovation for financial performance. The relevance of innovation for creating and capturing value is especially strong in the context of AI because the digital economy offers new opportunities and challenges for profiting from innovation. Here, the platform-based business models of companies in various sectors, such as Amazon, Airbnb, and Uber, have received particular managerial attention, and all of these companies launched major AI initiatives many years ago. In particular, these initiatives are aimed at intelligently leveraging customer data as a basis for developing completely new businesses. As such, innovation is a primary driver of recent disruptive evolutions across different industries.

In addition, innovation is a major driver of a company's market capitalization which emphasizes the need for developing a digital future story to convince potential collaborators and investors of a company's positive long-term prospects. On this basis, various conceptual arguments and empirical findings have led to the development of an innovation-based view of company performance.[2] In particular, innovation may affect a firm's financial performance because it enables, for example, additional revenues from new products or higher margins from specific services and superior business models. This logic assumes a relatively direct link between innovation and financial performance through revenue growth and higher margins. In addition, innovation may affect financial performance more indirectly. Innovation activities may strengthen the image and reputation of a company and of its products and solutions. In turn, this positive image and reputation may enable the company to achieve superior financial results, for example based on a higher brand value than competitors' brands.

This indirect link between innovation and financial performance focuses on external perceptions of a company's innovativeness, and it is particularly important in the context of AI. On the one hand, being among the leaders in using AI may impact a company's reputation for innovation. On the other hand, AI is often applied internally without the customers knowing about it. If a company is innovative – and if it is perceived as being innovative – its innovation activities may have an even higher return because of the indirect link on financial performance, for example by strengthening a company's reputation and brand. Therefore, it usually pays off to be considered innovative, and many companies like Apple and Amazon actually put considerable emphasis on their innovation communication. Even if many of their innovations derive from close collaborations with a variety of external partners, the communication of new product launches typically highlights the internal innovation strength of the organizations.

In light of the high importance of innovation perceptions in the context of AI, there are rankings of the most innovative companies in many countries. In addition, there are several well-known rankings of the world's most innovative companies. Many of these rankings are published by newspapers, magazines, and consultancies, and these rankings are often based on a combination of expert opinions along with some additional quantitative data. Every year, for example, the rankings of the world's most innovative companies by Forbes and MIT Technology Review as well as the Boston Consulting Group receive strong managerial and public attention. Because of the considerable differences in the methods and results of these rankings, a meta-ranking of the world's most innovative companies may shed new light on the importance of AI for innovation and corporate performance. A meta-ranking is more robust because it integrates the results of multiple rankings of the world's most innovative companies, and its findings may underscore the importance of external perceptions of innovativeness and of an intelligence-based view on corporate performance, including AI, HI, and a meta-intelligence.

Based on the high relevance of perceived innovativeness, a meta-ranking is a step towards a consistent understanding of which companies actually are among the most innovative – according to external experts and in light of the growing importance of AI. In fact, the innovation activities of many firms now include a substantial portion of digital innovation and AI. While the focus on digital innovation and AI has long been a fact for companies from the information and communications sector, it now also applies to many from traditional industrial sectors, such as machinery, automotive, retail, and many more. In many companies in these sectors, strategic initiatives for innovation, AI, and digital transformation are increasingly inseparable. In the initial wave of digital transformation, many executives have focused on capturing efficiency gains. Now, many companies focus on digital innovation to generate completely new solutions in order to achieve growth opportunities and new revenue streams. Here, AI plays a particularly prominent role. Thus, the relevance of AI for innovation output and impact has strongly increased in recent years.

How can we identify the world's most innovative companies?

If you are not interested in the underlying methods for identifying the most innovative firms based on a meta-ranking, please skip this section and move on to the results for the most innovative firms. To generate a meta-ranking of the world's most innovative companies, the results of five existing innovation rankings were used which have received considerable public attention by the innovation and AI community. Each of these rankings is published annually and includes at least 50 companies which are considered the most innovative worldwide. If more than 50 companies were listed in a ranking, only the top 50 companies were considered for the meta-ranking to ensure a high level of comparability across the different rankings. The information about these rankings was collected online in 2018. Since general innovation perceptions provide the basis for most of the rankings, they consider different types of innovation activities, including AI and beyond. Only the fourth ranking focuses specifically on technological innovations, which typically emphasize product and process innovations.

The first of the five rankings is entitled 'The most innovative companies 2018' and was published by the Boston Consulting Group.[3] According to the description of the study's methods, the ranking is based on a survey of senior executives from firms in various sectors worldwide. These survey results are complemented by an analysis of selected financial indicators, particularly total shareholder return.

The second ranking is entitled 'The world's most innovative companies 2018' and was published by Forbes magazine[4]. According to the methodological information provided in the article about the ranking, the order of the companies is determined by their innovation premium, i.e. the difference of market capitalization and net present value of existing business cash flows. These metrics are calculated with an algorithm from Credit Suisse HOLT. To be eligible for the ranking, seven years of public financial data are required as well as 10 billion US dollars in market capitalization, and the companies need to be active in sectors with quantifiable R&D expenditures, excluding, for example, financial services firms. For some companies, the ranking includes individual business units or regional units. Specifically, Unilever was mentioned twice with Hindustan Unilever and Unilever Indonesia. On this basis, only the higher rank was considered for the entire company Unilever.

The third ranking is entitled 'The world's most innovative companies 2018' and was published by Fast Company magazine.[5] According to the information provided for this ranking, more than 30 editors and contributors of the magazine surveyed thousands of companies in 36 categories. Many of them had been identified by means of a public submission process. The target and focus of the analyses was to identify the most important innovations of the previous year. On this basis, the innovations' impact on businesses, sectors, and the larger culture was studied. As a result of this analysis process, the most innovative companies overall and for different sectors were identified.

The fourth ranking is entitled 'The world's 50 most innovative companies' in 2018 and was published by USA Today based on an analysis of 24/7 Wall St.[6] According to the information provided in the article about the ranking, it draws on patent data analyses. In particular, it relies on information from patent research company IFI Claims Patent Services. The U.S. Patent and Trademark Office granted firms more than 320,000 patents in the previous year. As many patents belong to the same parent organization, 24/7 Wall St. combined patents for the same parent firm in order to identify the world's 50 most innovative companies. Each company in this ranking was granted at least 700 patents in the previous year, the top companies were granted thousands. In fact, a very limited number of firms account for a large share of patents. More specifically, 50 firms, including Apple, Google, Microsoft, and Amazon, accounted for about 30 percent of patents.

The fifth ranking is entitled the '50 smartest companies 2017' and was published by MIT Technology Review.[7] It was the most recent edition of this ranking at the time of collecting the information for the meta-ranking in 2018. According to the information given in the article about this ranking, the editors of the magazine every year select those firms that excel at integrating novel technologies with promising business models. In contrast to some of the other rankings, this ranking is not based on quantitative indicators, such as patents or R&D expenditures. There is no specific submission form, but the editors invite suggestions that may deserve to be included. Some companies in the ranking are large established corporations, such as Amazon and IBM, but the list also includes relatively new companies and startups.

To generate the meta-ranking, the results of the five individual rankings were aggregated. For cross-validation purposes, this aggregation was done in three ways. The first and most basic aggregation method is to consider the number of times that a company is included in a ranking. If the company is included in a ranking, this measure is 1, otherwise 0. Accordingly, the specific position in a ranking (between rank 1 and 50) is not taken into account. The minimum value for this first aggregation method is 0 points, whereas the maximum value is 5 points, which would refer to a company that is included in all five rankings.

The second aggregation method considers the specific rank between 1 and 50. To calculate a measure that indicates a higher position with a larger number of points, a firm's position in a ranking was transformed according to the following formula: number of points = 51 − original rank. Thus, the company in the first place of a ranking receives 50 points, whereas the company placed 50th receives 1 point. If a company is not included in a ranking, it receives 0 points. Accordingly, the minimum value for this second aggregation method is 0 points, whereas the maximum value is 250 points if a single company were to score the top rank in each of the five rankings.

The third aggregation method further considers the particular value of the top positions in a ranking. This approach acknowledges the specific challenges of achieving a ranking among the top 10 companies rather than the top 50 companies. Accordingly, this method does not assume an equal distance between the ranks in each ranking. In fact, there are not any absolute or relative numbers given as a basis for the ranking results in most of the five rankings. Therefore, this is assumed in the third aggregation method. Here, the number of points increases by 1 for the bottom 10 firms in each ranking. Thus, 50th place receives 1 point, whereas 41st place receives 10 points. Then, the number of points increases by 2 for the next 10 firms. Accordingly, 40th place receives 12 points, and 31st place receives 30 points. Afterwards, the number of points increases by 3 for the next 10 firms. Thus, 30th place receives 33 points, and 21st place receives 60 points. For the subsequent 10 firms, the number of points increases by 4. Consequently, 20th place receives 64 points, and 11st place receives 100 points. For the top 10 firms, the number of points increases by 5 for each place. Accordingly, 10th place receives 105 points, and 1st place receives 150 points. On this basis, scoring 1st place and 50th place in two rankings (150 + 1 = 151 points) is worth more than scoring places 25 and 26 (48 + 45 = 93 points). If a company is not ranked in a particular ranking, it receives 0 points. Thus, the minimum value for this third aggregation method is 0 points, and the maximum value is 750 points if a single company were to reach first place in each of the five rankings.

The results of the meta-ranking are quite robust in cross-validation analyses with these three different aggregation methods. Nonetheless, several limitations of the meta-ranking are worth noting. First, the meta-ranking depends on the five individual rankings and their methodological procedures. In this regard, some rankings only consider a subset of all companies, for instance based on the availability of multiple years of public financial data. Second, the underlying rankings partly exclude some sectors. For example, the Forbes ranking does not consider financial services firms. Hence, it is more difficult for companies from these sectors to achieve a high position in the meta-ranking. Third, the ranking by USA Today focuses exclusively on the patent position of innovating companies. However, the importance of patents for innovation strongly differs among industrial sectors, and these sector differences may also affect the results of the meta-ranking. Fourth, the relative dominance of US companies in the top positions of the meta-ranking may partly derive from the fact that all five individual rankings are published in the US although these rankings claim to include the most innovative companies worldwide. Fifth, the aggregation method has some influence on the results of the meta-ranking. While the three aggregation methods lead to largely consistent findings, minor differences in the scores of individual companies should be examined cautiously. Sixth, the analysis does not empirically examine performance relationships of the ranking results.

Which are the world's most innovative firms?

A surprising initial finding of the meta-ranking is the large number of companies that are among the 50 most innovative companies in at least one of the five rankings. Specifically, 203 different companies are part of the five top 50 rankings which led to a theoretical maximum of exactly 249 places since two different regional units of Unilever had been included in the Forbes ranking.[8] Thus, there are only very limited overlaps among the five rankings. Rather than providing a relatively consistent under-standing of the world's 50 most innovative companies, the different meth-odological approaches and strategic focus of the five rankings lead to very divergent lists of companies. In fact, only the 31 companies listed in Table 1 are mentioned in at least two of the five rankings. The points for the first aggregation method show that only eleven companies are included in at least three of the rankings. Two companies are part of four rankings, and only one is mentioned in all five rankings.

Rank	Company	Points Method 1	Points Method 2	Points Method 3
1	Amazon	5	225	625
2	Apple	4	174	472
3	Tencent	4	154	389
4	Google/Alphabet	3	140	400
5	Netflix	3	133	367
6	SpaceX	3	125	329
7	Tesla	3	114	300
8	Microsoft	3	114	287
9	IBM	3	105	279
10	Intel	3	105	257
11	General Electric	3	76	148

Rank	Company	Points Method 1	Points Method 2	Points Method 3
12	Samsung	2	95	275
13	Regeneron Pharma	2	83	215
14	Toyota	2	77	186
15	LG Electronics	2	71	179
16	Unilever	2	73	177
17	Facebook	2	72	174
18	Salesforce	2	54	154
19	Marriott	2	63	132
20	Illumina	2	62	129
21	Alibaba	2	51	115
22	Hewlett-Packard	2	52	104
23	Siemens	2	55	102
24	Cisco Systems	2	49	96
25	AT&T	2	46	75
26	DJI	2	42	70
27	Huawei	2	36	65
28	Expedia	2	37	61
29	Adidas	2	29	38
30	Daimler	2	23	31
31	Philips	2	9	9

Table 1: Results of the meta-ranking
(Source: Lichtenthaler, 2018, Journal of Strategy and Management[9])

The limited consistency of the results of the five rankings of the most innovative companies worldwide is one major finding of this meta-ranking. Therefore, the first aggregation method may actually be considered the most important approach because being mentioned in multiple rankings is a strong signal of innovativeness since the overlaps between the ranking results are so limited. Accordingly, Table 1 lists the top companies based on their points for the first aggregation method. On this basis, Amazon leads the meta-ranking based on five points for the first aggregation method. There are also two clear runners-up with Apple and Tencent being mentioned in four rankings. Then, the following eight companies result in a clear top 11 for the meta-ranking based on being mentioned in three rankings: Google/Alphabet, Netflix, SpaceX, Tesla, Microsoft, IBM, Intel, and General Electric. Interestingly, the group with three points for the first aggregation method comprises four firms, which are relatively young technology companies, i. e. Google/Alphabet, Netflix, SpaceX, and Tesla, as well as four firms, which are large and more established companies, i. e. Microsoft, IBM, Intel, and General Electric.

To understand the underlying reasons for the ranking results, two of the rankings, i. e. the third ranking by Fast Company magazine and the fifth ranking by MIT Technology Review, provide more detailed information for the companies that are included beyond the patent counts in the fourth ranking by USA Today. This brief information gives some more specific insights into why the companies are considered innovative. Here, a relatively strong focus of the arguments in the MIT Technology Review ranking on digital transformation and AI topics needs to be taken into account. This particular focus further underscores the importance of AI for innovation at present.

On this basis, the following information is given for the top 11 companies. Amazon is primarily considered because of its enormous presence in different fields and its strong competencies in AI. In a similar vein, Apple is assumed to deliver the future today in various areas, including AI. Tencent is highly regarded for its large user base and for honoring content as key. With respect to Google/Alphabet, its key role in AI is highlighted. Netflix is mentioned with regard to changing its industry and mastering different sizes of screens. SpaceX is included for putting outer space within reach. For Tesla, the focus is on its bold plans, such as the giant factory. For Microsoft, the strong role of the cloud business is underscored. Concerning IBM, the applications of blockchain technology and AI are highlighted. Similarly, AI is mentioned with regard to Intel, while the focus for General Electric is on industrial analytics, which is also strongly related to AI.

Accordingly, 9 of the top 11 companies in the meta-ranking are considered to be highly innovative because of their strong activities related to AI. Specifically, 5 of the top 11 companies, i. e. Amazon, Apple, Google/Alphabet, IBM, and Intel, are included in the underlying innovation rankings directly due to their strong role in AI. Moreover, 2 of the top 11 companies, i. e. Microsoft and General Electric, are mentioned with regard to technologies that are related to AI, such as industrial analytics, or that provide the basis for profiting from AI, e. g. cloud technologies. Finally, 2 of the top 11 companies, i. e. Tencent and Netflix, are included in the rankings, among other reasons, because they successfully leverage customer data for new solutions, strongly drawing on underlying AI. Only for 2 of the top 11 companies, i. e. SpaceX and Tesla, is AI not mentioned as a key factor determining their ranking. The primary reason for the innovative reputation of these two firms can rather be traced back to their disruption of established industries.

In contrast to the limited consistency of the results of the five rankings, the three aggregation methods for the meta-ranking lead to very consistent results. Specifically, 9 of the top 11 companies are identical according to each of the aggregation methods. As expected, the ranking is dominated by US companies, with 19 out of the 31 top companies from the US. While this indicates the innovative strength of US companies, the origin of the five rankings, which are all compiled in the US, may also play a role. In addition, four Chinese companies are considered among the top innovators with Tencent in 3rd place, Alibaba in 21st place, DJI 26th place, and Huawei in 27th place. Three companies are from Germany, i. e. Siemens (23rd), Adidas (29th), and Daimler (30th), and two from South Korea, i. e. Samsung (12th) and LG (15th). The list of the top 31 companies is completed with one company from Japan (Toyota, 14th), one from the Netherlands (Philips, 31st), and one from the UK/Netherlands (Unilever, 16th).

With regard to the industry distribution of the most innovative companies, there are many 'technology' companies among the top firms, including the top 3, i.e. Amazon, Apple, and Tencent. Overall, however, there is quite some diversity with respect to different sectors, including automotive firms, such as Toyota and Daimler, as well as industrial giants, such as General Electric and Siemens. Among the top 31 companies, there are also several 'digital natives', such as Facebook and Netflix, but also well established firms from other sectors, such as Adidas and Unilever. In addition, two companies that have been decisively shaped by a single individual, i.e. Elon Musk, are part of the top ten, with SpaceX on rank 6 and Tesla on rank 7. With regard to innovation beyond AI, many of the companies do not focus exclusively on product innovation, but they are also well known for service innovation and particularly business model innovation based on the information given in the articles about the rankings. On this basis, several of the companies are well known for successful transformation processes and/or for disrupting their industries, e.g. Amazon, Netflix, and SpaceX.

What importance does AI have for the most innovative firms?

The findings of the meta-ranking have several important implications. First, the results underscore the relevance of innovation perceptions. In particular, the meta-ranking shows the distinct findings of the five underlying rankings. While all of these five rankings claim to identify the world's most innovative companies, their results are very different based on distinct procedures and strategic focus in preparing the rankings. The results of the individual rankings vary strongly, and apart from a key role of AI there does not appear to be a lot of agreement which 50 companies specifically are the most innovative companies in the world. This surprisingly low consistency of the individual rankings can be interpreted as a strong signal for the diversity of ways in which a company can innovate – and for the diversity of ways in which a company may be considered innovative. In contrast to the limited consistency of the individual rankings, the different aggregation methods for generating the meta-ranking lead to very consistent results. Thus, it is possible to arrive at a convincing list of the most innovative companies with different methods based on the results of the five underlying rankings. Due to the consistent results of the cross-validation analyses with the three aggregation methods, the results of the meta-ranking help to understand which firms are perceived as the leading innovators. While the perception of a company as being among the top innovators in a single ranking varies strongly across multiple rankings, the aggregation methods lead to consistent findings. If there is one major driver in the perception of a firm as innovative, it clearly is a strong role in AI and related fields.

Second, the findings of the meta-ranking provide new insights into the importance of different types of innovation, which together lead to strong perceptions of innovativeness. Based on the articles about the five rankings, most of the top companies in the meta-ranking share a leading role in the development and application of AI. On this basis, the top companies are well known for product innovation and service innovation, whereas process innovation and other innovation types seem to play a less important role in public perception. Arguably most important, however, for an innovative public perception is business model innovation based on AI and digital technology. Many companies in the ranking, including Amazon and Apple, are well known for convincing customers with new digital business models. These business models are often considered superior by customers relative to established business models. Consequently, the new business models have played a key role for the companies becoming financially successful. In many cases, the new business models are complementary to other types of innovation, such as product innovation and service innovation.

Third, the results of the meta-ranking highlight the relevance of renewing a company's innovation activities over time as a basis for innovative public perceptions. For instance, SpaceX and Netflix are well known for disrupting established industries based on transformative innovation activities. Most other companies among the top 11 firms are well known for their AI activities, especially Amazon, Apple, Tencent, Google/Alphabet, Microsoft, IBM, and Intel. Thus, there may be a lot of additional potential in terms of disruptive innovation based on AI, which is currently not achieved by many companies even if they are relatively innovative in other ways. Thus, the importance of innovation is high today, and it may even further increase in the future. One major reason for this expected further increase is the continuing evolution towards AI which calls for developing completely new solutions besides optimizing existing products and processes to achieve higher levels of efficiency. In this regard, a systematic innovation management enables companies to capture value from digital innovation and AI because innovation, digitalization, and AI are increasingly inseparable in many firms, and the particular importance of digital innovation and AI is likely to continue over the next years.

Fourth, the findings of the meta-ranking illustrate how the generation of new markets leads to external perceptions of innovativeness. The top companies according to the meta-ranking comprise old companies in established industries, such as General Electric and Daimler, as well as relatively young companies from growth sectors. These relatively young companies, such as Tencent and Netflix, have grown very rapidly in recent years, and a lot of this substantial growth may be attributed to creating completely new markets for their products and services, at least in their respective regions. The leading companies in these new markets are considered particularly innovative, and this public perception helps them to sustain their innovation-based competitive advantage over time. Accordingly, they are able to keep their innovative pace while transitioning from start-ups on the markets to corporate entrepreneurship in large companies.

Finally, the results of the meta-ranking offer new insights into capturing value from innovation in the context of digital transformation and AI. Overall, there are companies from many different sectors among the most innovative firms according to the meta-ranking. Thus, the ranking is not exclusively dominated by 'technology' companies that focus on software and IT. Nonetheless, a significant part of the leading innovators has a business model emphasizing digital platforms, which are strengthened by means of AI. These companies are 'digital natives', and they dominate a large part of their markets based on offering an essential platform, e. g. Amazon and Facebook. Digital innovations and AI now play a significant role in the innovation activities of most large companies, but the prominent position of these leading digital innovators further highlights the complementarity of multiple types of digital innovations, including multi-sided platforms as a new business model. In addition, the findings underscore the need for developing an intelligence-based view towards understanding competitive advantage in the digital economy.

Part B
Framework

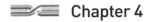 Chapter 4

An intelligence-based view of company performance

How a company may achieve a competitive advantage and superior performance is at the very heart of business strategy.[1] More specifically, a company's ability to gain a competitive advantage at one point and to further sustain it over time may be considered the holy grail of strategic management. Consequently, multiple schools of thought have addressed these key issues. Over the past decades, these different conceptual frameworks have received varying degrees of attention with each perspective partly balancing the strengths and weaknesses of other perspectives. It is possible to draw a general distinction between externally and internally oriented views of understanding and analyzing company performance. Popular perspectives with a focus on external factors are the industrial organization perspective and the five forces framework for competitive strategy.[2] Here, the logic follows the basic idea that those firms will be successful that are competitively well-positioned in an attractive industry.

In contrast to these externally driven perspectives, several frameworks with a focus on internal factors have received considerable attention. In particular, the resource-based and competence-based perspectives need to be mentioned here.[3] Basically, these strategy frameworks assume that those companies will be most successful that accumulate valuable resources, which provide the basis for developing relevant competencies and capabilities. Critical competencies may become core competencies, which are hard to imitate for competitors. These competencies and capabilities may help businesses to achieve a competitive advantage. Beyond gaining a competitive advantage at one point, companies ideally should be able to rejuvenate this competitive advantage over time to enjoy superior performance for a longer period. In light of an increasingly dynamic competitive environment in most sectors, the dynamic capabilities and innovation-based perspectives put particular emphasis on those activities and capabilities that are needed for dynamically sustaining a competitive advantage.[4]

While some arguments of the externally and internally oriented strategy frameworks are contradictory, many parts are complementary because they draw managerial attention to different components that may be influenced by a company's executives. An exclusive focus on external market-related strategy variables will most likely be insufficient for achieving a significant competitive advantage today. At the same time, a pure focus on internal resources and capabilities may be insufficient for fully leveraging these competencies in the marketplace. Finally, exclusive attention to dynamic perspectives, such as the dynamic capabilities and innovation-based views, may overemphasize the continuous adaptation of organizations while deemphasizing some of the other critical variables. Taken together, these strategy frameworks have provided important insights, especially when several of these perspectives are used to examine a particular firm's situation from multiple different perspectives.

With regard to AI, however, the suitability of these frameworks can only be called mixed. The externally oriented strategy frameworks help us to understand the changing competition that may emerge from the advances in AI. In contrast, the internally oriented strategy frameworks indicate that the proficient development and application of AI solutions may be considered a specific organizational capability – and potentially a core competence. In addition, the frameworks emphasizing the dynamic adaptation of companies, such as the innovation-based view, underscore the importance of transforming a company's business activities in light of major advances in the field of AI and related technologies. Thus, existing strategy frameworks allow for accommodating the recent evolution of AI, but they do not enable executives to fully map the competitive consequences of AI and its interplay with a firm's human expertise. These interrelationships and their impact on company performance cannot be examined comprehensively with established strategy frameworks. Rather, a distinctly intelligence-based view of company performance provides important new insights.

In this regard, some important academic groundwork was done about three decades ago. Along with a growing importance of knowledge management in companies, the notion of a knowledge-based view of business was developed in the 1990s.[5] Basically, it is an extension of the resource-based perspective because it considers knowledge as the key resource of companies. Knowledge is often complex and difficult to imitate, especially if it is tacit knowledge, which may not be easy to articulate. Therefore, knowledge may provide an important basis for achieving a competitive advantage because it may be challenging for competitors to reduce major differences in the knowledge bases among firms. In addition, the knowledge-based view enables detailed analyses of how electronic knowledge management systems may contribute to company performance by helping to share information and knowledge within companies and across organizational boundaries. While the knowledge-based view has substantially clarified the competitive impact of knowledge and of knowledge management systems, it does not fully incorporate the role of intelligence, either human or artificial.

From a knowledge-based to an intelligence-based view

The knowledge-based view has provided important insights into how companies may achieve a competitive advantage by developing particular knowledge from underlying information and data. In this regard, data usually describes certain discrete elements, such as numbers and words. If the data is organized, structured and useful, it becomes information, which refers to linked elements, such as equations or sentences. If information is given meaning by beeing contextualized, organized and synthesized, it becomes knowledge, for example chapters or theories. There are other systematizations of data, information, and knowledge, but this is an understanding that is consistent with the knowledge-based view of company performance. Basically, the knowledge-centered strategy framework suggests that the possibilities for obtainig a competitive advantage from data and information are limited, whereas the step from information to knowledge is key because the synthesized and organized knowledge in a particular context is too complex and challenging for competitors to thoroughly understand and copy it.

Beyond gaining a competitive advantage due to different knowledge bases, however, businesses may also achieve superior performance because of a unique intelligence architecture, including their human and artificial intelligence. In this regard, intelligence may be regarded as the next step beyond knowledge that enables wisdom. Specifically, knowledge becomes intelligence if it is given insight and enables understanding because it is integrated and actionable. Following the analogy of words, sentences, and chapters – referring to data, information, and knowledge – an example for intelligence could be a book. Drawing on the analogy of numbers, equations, and theories, an example for intelligence could be a system or paradigm. Thus, intelligence describes knowledge that is applied and further organized to enable particular insights that could not be gained from the knowledge itself without any particular intelligence. As such, the intelligence-based view is an evolution of the knowledge-based view.

At first glance, these conceptual distinctions may appear to be relevant only academically. However, they also have immediate practical implications for strategic management. In particular, an intelligence-based view underscores that firms with the same knowledge may have significantly different performance outcomes. Even if two companies have access to the same internal and external knowledge, they may attain completely different competitive positions if one firm has a superior intelligence that enables specific insights as a basis for targeted competitive moves that the other firm lacks. These intelligence-based advantages may derive from human or artificial intelligence – or from a combination of the two. Independent of the particular type of intelligence, these performance discrepancies may not be explained with a mere knowledge-based strategy framework.

For instance, imagine two companies becoming aware of new technological developments based on comprehensive technology foresight activities. Both of these companies gain some new knowledge about technological developments. The company with a superior level of intelligence may generate valuable insights from this additional knowledge, and these insights may enable the firm to arrive at new products and services drawing on the new technologies which open up a novel market. The competitive advantage in the market is based on the company's intelligence because the two firms in this illustrative example had at their disposal similar data, information, and knowledge. Accordingly, the example shows an important contribution of an intelligence-based view beyond knowledge-based arguments. Here, it is critical to note that this basic example does not require particular AI solutions to illustrate the value of an intelligence-based strategy framework.

These conceptual arguments help to clarify why different types of intelligence are competitively relevant beyond particular knowledge bases. To achieve a sustainable competitive advantage, it is therefore key for companies to develop particular types of intelligence that their existing and potential competitors lack. Despite the critical role of intelligence, however, an intelligence-based view of company performance does not imply that data, information, and knowledge are not important. Rather, knowledge is also key according to the intelligence-based understanding of strategy. If, hypothetically, companies only had intelligence without any underlying knowledge, they would continually develop similar types of knowledge. Basically, a company with a high level of intelligence – human and/or artificial – would start unnecessarily reinventing different concepts, processes, and other things without being able to achieve the benefits from the knowledge bases that its competitors have probably already developed. Accordingly, developing high levels of intelligence without any underlying knowledge is not useful from a competitive point of view.

Human and artificial intelligence

Intelligence can be defined in a wide variety of ways. Basically, it involves some mental activities, such as learning, reasoning, understanding, seeing relationships, and more. While algorithms and data analytics solutions can be used to enable some kind of AI, no computer has so far been able entirely to implement any of these mental activities. Nonetheless, there have been major advances in different fields of AI in recent years. Consequently, it is helpful to reach a systematic understanding of what kinds of intelligence a human typically has and whether these mental activities may potentially be simulated at some point in the foreseeable future. Particular types of HI already provide an important basis for competitive advantage. Specifically, some companies, such as Google and many consulting firms, place a strong emphasis on selecting candidates in hiring processes based on selected indicators for different types of intelligence. An intelligence-based view of company performance enables executives to highlight the HI of their employees as a particular competitive strength.

There are various reasons for assuming a positive performance impact of HI. In particular, HI may have direct and indirect effects on company performance. In this regard, HI may lead directly to better results. For example, different types of HI may help to make more informed managerial decisions, which positively affect subsequent performance. In a similar vein, particular engineering skills of human experts may contribute to solutions that are superior to competitors' products, leading to a competitive advantage that can quite easily be traced back to human expertise – even if intelligence leads to superior products only, which then provide the basis for enhanced performance. Beyond these relatively direct benefits, however, HI may contribute to better decisions in selecting new employees, in wisely spending budgets, or in choosing the right partners for a strategic alliance or M&A deal.

All of these key strategic variables are strongly affected by the intelligence of the humans that are involved in the specific topics and decisions. Thus, the overall impact of HI goes far beyond a few amazing ideas and extraordinary talents of selected employees. In particular, HI also affects the choice of AI applications. Specifically, the appropriate application of

AI partly depends on the managerial decision to rely on AI for that particular application. Consequently, the impact of HI on company performance may be broader and stronger than you may initially assume, even if the growing relevance of AI is taken into account. While this impact may take many different forms and follow a relatively long chain of effects, it may often be traced back to particular types of HI. There have been multiple attempts to systematize HI. A detailed review would exceed the scope of this chapter, but the following classification of Howard Gardner of Harvard University has become a well-accepted overview of different types of HI.[6] Specifically, the distinction is part of the theory of multiple intelligences, which differentiates HI into specific modalities rather than viewing it as one overall ability. Specifically, the theory distinguishes seven types of human intelligence, with different potential for simulation by means of computers.

The first type of HI is bodily-kinesthetic intelligence, which refers to the control of bodily motions and the ability to carefully handle objects. This type of intelligence may be imitated by robots, even if they only perform repetitive tasks. The second type of HI is creative intelligence, which refers to developing new patterns of thought that enable unique artistic, musical, or written output. The third type of HI refers to interpersonal intelligence, which describes a human's sensitivity to others' feelings and the ability to work together in a group. Thus, this type of intelligence is related to notions of emotional intelligence. The fourth type of HI is intrapersonal intelligence, and it refers to inward-looking and self-reflective capabilities. It enables a person to develop a thorough understanding of the self and of one's strengths and weaknesses. As such, it currently is a human-only type of intelligence. The fifth type of HI is linguistic intelligence, and it describes a strong ability with words and languages. This type of intelligence includes, for example, understanding written and spoken input, processing this input, and providing a useful and understandable answer. The sixth type of HI is logical-mathematical intelligence, and it refers to logic, reasoning, numbers, and abstractions. Thus, it enables calculating results, exploring patterns and drawing comparisons. Finally, the seventh type of HI is visual-spatial intelligence, which describes spatial judgment and the ability to visualize in physical environments.[7]

In addition to these seven types of HI, some other types have been suggested by Howard Gardner and others, including existential, naturalistic, and a teaching-pedagogical intelligence. However, the focus here is on the original seven types of HI because even adding several more will most likely not lead to an exhaustive list of intelligence types. From a strategic management perspective, it further is not essential what particular segmentation of HI is used. For achieving a competitive advantage, it rather is more important that a company – or its employees – have the particular ability and that the firm knows how to best make use of this ability. This application of a specific type of HI may occur in relative isolation or it may occur in combination with one or multiple types of AI. Comparable to many different categorizations of HI, there are also many different conceptual frameworks and overviews of various types of AI. In fact, besides multiple different definitions of AI, there are probably even more categorizations of different types of AI.

Here, it is particularly important to remember that the understanding of AI is dynamic and changing over time. AI generally refers to theory and computer systems that are able to perform tasks that usually would call for HI. Over time, however, some of the AI applications become standard, and such routine automation is no longer called AI. Within the overall field of what is considered AI today, the topic of machine learning has probably received the most public attention in recent years. Machine learning typically relies on algorithms and statistical techniques that enable computer systems to progressively improve their performance in carrying out a particular task. In this regard, machine learning relies on underlying training data, which enables the system to make predictions without being specifically programmed to complete the task. A further subset of machine learning is deep learning, which refers to learning data representations instead of focused and task-specific algorithms.

Another important classification distinguishes four different types of AI: reactive machines, limited memory, theory of mind, and self-awareness. Reactive machines do not have any memory or experience. Instead, they rely on smart algorithms and massive computational power. Limited memory systems rely on some level of memory to build on experience for different situations. This enables the system to reduce reaction time in making new decisions. Theory of mind refers to systems that consider their own goals as well as potentially interfering goals of other entities. This kind of understanding is possible today, but its business applications are still limited. Finally, self-awareness describes systems that have an understanding of self and some consciousness. This would be the type of AI that is imagined in movies and some future scenarios.[8] While the distinction of these four types of AI is important, it includes several fields that are not central for competition in the near to medium future. Therefore, it may be more suitable to focus on various types of AI based on different applications and use cases of the underlying technologies. In this respect, the following classification is helpful from a strategic management point of view, although the different types of AI are not a hundred percent mutually exclusive. For example, machine learning also provides the basis for some other applications that are considered different categories. Nonetheless, the distinction of the following seven types is particularly helpful for discussing the competitive implications of the interactions of AI with HI.

The first type of AI consists of expert systems, which are directed at imitating the decision-making of a human expert. Typically, these systems comprise an underlying knowledge base with facts and rules as well as the inference engine that applies the rules. The second type of AI refers to machine learning, which includes for example deep learning and predictive analytics as core topics. The third type of AI involves various technologies that enable natural language processing. Here, the focus is on extracting, grouping, and categorizing information as well as translation and related applications. The fourth type of AI describes planning and scheduling systems, which refer to the development of action strategies and sequences for subsequent execution. Typically, the emphasis is on complex solutions in a multidimensional space. The fifth type of AI refers to robotics and machines. To further segment this field, we can again draw on the distinction of reactive machines, limited memory, theory of mind, and self-awareness. The sixth type of AI refers to speech synthesis systems, which include both directions of text-to-speech and speech-to-text solutions. Finally, the seventh type of AI refers to the topic of computer vision, and it comprises image recognition, machine vision, and related applications.[9]

Applications of these different types of AI may replace human work to some degree. However, this separate use of AI and HI is only one way in which businesses may profit from the recent advances in AI technologies. In particular, replacing human work primarily enables companies to capture efficiency gains. While these benefits may have important positive effects on financial performance, they are only one facet of leveraging AI. If companies attempt to additionally develop novel solutions as a basis for further growth and business development, they often need to combine one or multiple types of AI with one or multiple types of HI. For example, enhanced algorithms for predicting customer behavior may be combined with human creativity to enable completely new business models. Thus, it is important to distinguish the augmentation of HI from completely independent tasks that may be performed by AI. Beyond the example of an algorithm, you may also think about a surgical device that includes AI to enhance a surgeon's physical ability versus a robot that is able to make fully independent movements. These essential interactions of AI and HI are addressed more thoroughly in chapter 5.

The distinct types of HI and AI are at the core of the intelligence-based view of company performance. This is shown in the conceptual framework in Figure 2. By developing and applying the different types of intelligence – while considering their interdependencies – firms may gain a competitive advantage relative to other firms that do not possess similar levels of the particular types of intelligence. In this regard, AI and HI draw on the underlying data, information, and knowledge. Without these underlying components, which form a firm's knowledge base, the value of most types of intelligence would be relatively limited. Consider, for example, any algorithm for predictive maintenance. Without meaningful input data, even the most advanced version of this type of AI would provide hardly any value. In a similar vein, a human's interpersonal intelligence will provide limited benefits in the absence of any underlying information and knowledge. Accordingly, AI and HI build on the underlying knowledge base. In turn, the application of the distinct types of intelligence leads to the development of further data, information, and knowledge. Thus, a company strengthens its knowledge by accumulating and enhancing its different types of intelligence.

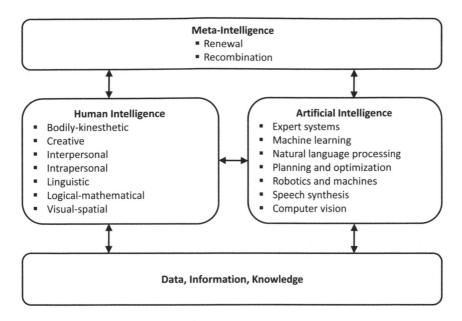

Figure 2: Framework for an intelligence-based view
(Source: Lichtenthaler, 2019, Journal of Innovation Management[10])

Along with the underlying data, information, and knowledge, the combination of HI and AI may provide an important basis for developing a competitive advantage. While a thorough understanding of these relations may be essential for executives because of the recent advances in AI, the multiple types of HI and AI only provide an initial step. Yes, it is essential to build up an intelligence-based competitive advantage at one moment. However, a firm's intelligence architecture may be excellent for achieving this competitive advantage today, but it will most probably be insufficient for keeping a strong competitive position in the future. Over time, a firm's intelligence-based advantage will inevitably deteriorate. With regard to HI, for example, key players may leave a company, which will need to find ways to replace or ideally more than compensate for the different types of intelligence that are lost with these key employees. Concerning AI, for example, a top position with regard to natural language processing today will not even be close to a top position in that field of AI in a few years' time because competitors are quickly catching up and the evolution of this entire field is extremely dynamic.

As such, even the highest level of some type of intelligence today will only enable a firm to gain a competitive advantage under the condition that it is strategically used for strengthening the firm's competitive position in an appropriate way. In contrast, it will be insufficient for sustaining this competitive advantage over time. Accordingly, firms not only need to strengthen their different types of AI and HI. Instead, they also need to develop a higher-order intelligence for dynamically transforming the different types of AI and HI in accordance with their strategies. This meta-intelligence includes the renewal and recombination of the different types of HI and AI. Thus, it enables the targeted transformation of a firm's intelligence architecture to reactively respond or to proactively shape the changing conditions of the competitive environment. Thus, the companies need Intelligence^X – which consists of various types of AI and HI as well as meta-intelligence. This essential role of meta-intelligence with regard to renewing and recombining a firm's multiple intelligences is addressed in more detail in chapter 6.

Implications of an intelligence-based view

An intelligence-based view has some important strategic implications. While the combination of AI and HI as well as meta-intelligence is addressed in more detail the next chapters, the basic framework of the intelligence-based view already provides a few essential insights. First, an intelligence-based view of company performance substantially advances the extant perspective of a knowledge-based view. In particular, it illustrates how different types of HI and AI may be developed and used in order to leverage the underlying knowledge, information, and data, which have been addressed in the knowledge-based perspective. As such, the focus on various types of intelligence further helps to understand major performance differences between firms with largely similar knowledge bases.

Specifically, knowledge per se may not enable a firm to achieve a competitive advantage unless it is exploited in a meaningful way according to a firm's corporate and business strategies. Therefore, the multiple intelligences provide a critical missing link between a firm's knowledge base and subsequent performance outcomes.

Second, the concept of intelligence architecture highlights the need for an integrated perspective on the different types of HI and AI, both of which draw on the underlying knowledge base. In this regard, the different types of intelligence underscore how a firm's knowledge base is developed because the multiple intelligences not only build on the underlying knowledge. Rather, they also contribute to the extension of the knowledge and to the generation of completely new knowledge. In particular, this understanding of a firm's entire intelligence architecture underscores the need for going beyond particular AI applications as isolated solutions. If executives aim to fully leverage the benefits of AI, they need to put the interfaces between those applications and the remaining parts of their firm's intelligence architecture at the centre of their attention. These interfaces will be critical for achieving a competitive advantage because they may not be imitated as easily as stand-alone AI solutions, whose potential impact on gaining a competitive advantage may decrease in the future because they will be mastered by many different competitors. In contrast, a company's complex intelligence architecture will remain a sound basis for a sustainable competitive advantage.

Third, an intelligence-based view provides new insights into the competitive effects of HI and human expertise. While superior human resources may play a major role in other frameworks for understanding company performance, such as the resource-based view and knowledge-based view, an intelligence focus offers a more thorough understanding how different types of HI may actually contribute to achieving a competitive advantage. The seven different types of HI go considerably beyond most previous analyses of human-centered superior company performance. In particular, the focus on different human intelligences enables systematic analyses of interdependencies with the variety of artificial intelligences. In this regard, it is particularly important to underscore the core role of HI despite the substantial advances of AI. There are manifold reasons for the continuing importance of HI, with one straightforward reason being often overlooked. Human experts select each particular application of AI in companies. However advanced AI technologies are today or may be in the future, they will still substantially depend on human expertise and intelligence to unfold any competitive impact. Thus, this minor example of the impact of HI on selecting AI applications underscores the importance of HI in an intelligence-based view of company performance – today and in the future.

Fourth, an intelligence-based perspective provides new insights into the strategic implications of utilizing AI. In particular, it offers a framework for systematically examining the direct and indirect consequences of multiple types of AI on company performance. Thus, it emphasizes the need for analyzing the interplay of AI applications with various types of HI in a particular situation. A specific AI application may positively affect competitive advantage if it is combined with a suitable type of HI. By contrast, the same AI application may provide hardly any benefit if it is not aligned with the remaining parts of a company's intelligence architecture. This key role of the internal organizational context in which AI is used has been overlooked quite often. In many situations, however, AI does not automatically contribute to higher performance. Instead, its strategic alignment in the organization is key to ensuring that the investments in AI actually pay off. The importance of considering a company's entire intelligence architecture will further grow in the future because particular AI applications will increasingly become standard tools, which may be used by many different companies at a nearly identical level of proficiency.

Fifth and finally, an intelligence-based view is inherently dynamic. The significant improvements in AI technologies in recent years emphasize the need for staying ahead of the competition in terms of developing, customizing, and applying the latest versions of AI. In light of the major dynamics of most firms' competitive environment in general and the advances of AI in particular, the continuous development and extension of a firm's HI becomes even more critical than in the past. In this regard, an intelligence-based view enables a comprehensive overview of a firm's intelligence architecture. Here, the various types of AI and HI provide immediate starting points for executives to adapt and to transform established competencies and experiences. Specifically, the concept of a meta-intelligence highlights the need for an ongoing transformation of the intelligence architecture. Without renewing HI and AI, any potential competitive advantage will be lost quite quickly. Besides renewing the intelligences, executives need to recombine the interrelationships among the different types of intelligence to ensure that the interfaces of HI and AI contribute to a firm's future competitive position.

 Chapter 5

Combining and complementing human and artificial intelligence

'Robots will kill at least about a third of our business.' This and similar statements are currently made by many business unit leaders of established insurance companies. Moreover, the employees in many of these companies fear substantial job cuts over the next years in light of the further development of AI and related technologies. In fact, executives in a range of industries, from machinery and electronics to retail and insurance, agree that AI has the potential to damage their established business lines substantially, leading to a significant loss of traditional jobs. At the same time, however, many knowledge workers, including those in R&D, feel unthreatened – the unique competencies required by creative work, they assert, are not replicable by AI. Therefore, they are quite relaxed with regard to their particular role in a future competitive environment that builds on a stronger use of AI. Even enthusiasts acknowledge the limitations of AI, now and for at least the next 10 years, if not well beyond this period.[1]

So who is right – the camp highlighting the potential of AI to replace humans or the camp arguing for the irreplaceable uniqueness of human intelligence? In fact, these two perspectives are parts of a more complex story. So far, no coherent perspective has emerged around these issues, either in academic studies or in more general discussions. Industry experts and consulting professionals also disagree about the likely consequences of AI. A large number of different studies come to surprisingly diverging results concerning the impact of AI on the number of human jobs in different industries. Some recent studies from a variety of organizations, including the OECD, the World Economic Forum, Forrester, and McKinsey, expect the advancement of AI to result in only a limited net loss of jobs if the new jobs AI will create are also taken into consideration. An article summarizing these studies suggests that it may still be too early to forecast the number of job cuts and new jobs, as well as their relative importance.[2]

In fact, the bulk of the attention given to AI in recent years has focused on the efficiency gains that could be reaped from advanced automation techniques based on intelligent algorithms, which have the capability to replace at least some human work. The potential for developing completely new solutions and achieving growth by combining human and artificial intelligence has received insufficient attention until very recently. Only slowly, executives have started to address the combinative benefits of integrating HI and AI. This strategic perspective considers human and artificial intelligence as complementary rather than competitive, and it may help to bridge the inconsistent results of previous studies, articles, and discussions.

4S framework for interplays of human and artificial intelligence

The relationship between human and artificial intelligence may be described in terms of a matrix that maps out four different interplays, each engaging different combinations of human and artificial intelligence. This leads to the 4S framework, which is illustrated in Figure 3. The first interplay is termed 'Standard', and it indicates activities that require limited levels of HI and AI. At this level of interplay, AI takes the lead. Standard procedures that have been automated for a substantial period of time and require low levels of either human or artificial intelligence are easily taken over by relatively low-level automation devices. For example, the robot-based automation of production processes in the automotive industry, e.g. at Ford or Mercedes, began decades ago. While these activities may have engaged with the latest AI technology when the automation process began, they are regarded as standard routines today.

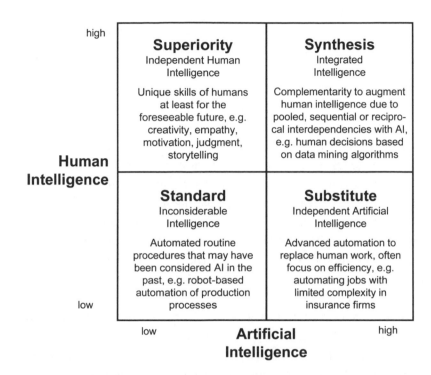

Figure 3: 4S framework for interplays of human and artificial intelligence (Source: Lichtenthaler, 2018, Research-Technology Management[3])

The second interplay is called 'Substitute' and involves high levels of AI and limited levels of HI. In this corner of the matrix, AI provides a substitute for HI. These kinds of developments have received the bulk of attention in recent discussions of AI. One example is the growing automation of jobs with limited complexity and easily defined skill levels in the insurance industry, such as the use of customer service bots in some customer interactions. Therefore, many leading insurance companies, such as MetLife and Allianz, have started initiatives which involve a stronger use of AI relative to HI, for example for streamlining the claims process. The focus of these kinds of activities is on enhancing efficiency and lowering costs by replacing human workers with AI.

The third interplay is termed 'Superiority', and it refers to the singularity of HI relative to AI in specific fields – at least in the foreseeable future. In this section of the matrix, HI dominates and will continue to do so for the near and medium future. Uniquely human skills, such as creativity, empathy, judgment, storytelling, and motivational speeches, are not (yet) easily replicable via AI.[4] This is the reason why people from creative disciplines working in large advertising agencies, such as the Omnicom Group, are still quite relaxed with regard to AI as potential competition. AI is used in these firms, and it may replace some jobs, but there is still a long way to go for AI technology to substitute the creative jobs. Moreover, it will be very difficult to replace human capabilities that feed creativity and inventiveness, such as knowing what questions to ask and imagining a thing that does not yet exist.[5] Nonetheless, the applications where independent HI outperforms AI will continue to shrink over the next years. This will put another key question at the center of executive attention: what will be – and should be – a company's human-based core competencies in a fully digital future?

Finally, the fourth interplay is called 'Synthesis' because it goes beyond viewing HI and AI as independent in order to focus on their synthesis for achieving integrated intelligence. In this domain, AI is used to augment— not replace—human intelligence; for instance, human decision making can be enhanced by information provided by data-mining algorithms. The partly automated business intelligence system developed by Conatix, for example, draws on machine learning technology to discover and structure external data and information that was previously unstructured. The algorithm works in close interaction with human researchers to update and realign its targets to deliver effective business intelligence insights.[6]

In the synthesis domain, human and artificial intelligence work together, creating a kind of integrated intelligence. In this scenario, AI will not eliminate human jobs but reshape them. This approach offers both completely new possibilities and intriguing new challenges for work systems design. Human-machine interaction and teamwork will enable different levels of autonomy, which will provide opportunities for developing completely new solutions that could not be supported by either human or artificial intelligence alone, or even by less integrated versions of this synthesis.[7] These new solutions provide additional value that may lead to new jobs and spur investments in further enhancing AI technology.

The synthesis domain may well be the ruling case in the field of radiology. Some AI enthusiasts have assumed that AI can replace radiologists in detecting pathologies in radiological images, but studies suggest that complete replacement is unlikely. Rather, the job profile of radiologists – the things they actually do – will change. For example, radiologists in the future will need to collaborate with and train AIs to support their work. As a result of this collaboration, the overall effectiveness of radiology services is expected to grow. AI will perform the routine tasks and provide data to support decision-making while radiologists will be needed for expert assessment and discussion of potential treatments with other physicians. In this way, AI will add value without replacing human intelligence. The extent of that value may be difficult to predict at this point. Integrated human and artificial intelligence can make possible completely novel solutions, and new value creation models. Indeed, major advances may require a collaborative interaction that uses AI to enhance human thinking and performance.[8]

The benefits of complementarity may be accessed through pooled, sequential, or reciprocal interdependence of human and artificial intelligence. In pooled interdependence, human and artificial intelligence provide distinct contributions that together produce a result that exceeds the sum of the parts. For example, financial investment decisions are enhanced by relying on both human analyses and the conclusions of AI-based data mining work. In sequential interdependence, the output of one type of intelligence is the basis for activities of the other type. For example, customer service bots may be used to respond to general questions from customers, who are then handed over to call center employees when their individual concerns extend beyond the AI's capabilities. Finally, reciprocal interdependence is cyclical. For instance, strategic planning processes may rely on multiple rounds of AI data mining interspersed with human analyses that direct subsequent AI efforts to fine-tune conclusions.

The different interplays between human and artificial intelligence are illustrated by recent AI initiatives at some large, established companies, among them General Electric and its German competitor Siemens. Both companies are among the world leaders in solutions in the standard realm, automating production processes. At the same time, General Electric and Siemens continue to invest heavily in outstanding HI and unique skills, for example in the fields of engineering, creativity, and storytelling, reflecting their need for experts in skills that cannot be replicated by AI – skills that fall into the superiority domain. Consequently, the companies' approaches to the standard and superiority domains have been highly optimized, with adjustments to innovation processes in both companies to enable higher levels of agility and flexibility to respond to the particular challenges of development projects with significant digital components.[9] AI initiatives at both General Electric and Siemens have been strengthened in the past few years. The companies have hired large numbers of AI experts, and they continue to develop internal competencies to leverage integrated insights of engineering and AI professionals. So far, a major focus of these initiatives has been on the substitute domain – making work more efficient by substituting AI effort for human effort.

Both companies have worked to optimize their clients' processes by means of AI based on underlying industrial Internet of Things platforms, such as General Electric's Predix and Siemens' MindSphere. As part of this effort, these companies have developed thousands of digital twins of buildings and complex machinery. These digital replicas allow engineers to make the buildings and machinery operate more efficiently by optimizing processes based on conclusions drawn from using machine learning to analyze vast flows of data from what had been completely siloed data signals.[10] Increasingly, however, both companies have begun to shift the emphasis of their AI activities to developing new solutions that lead to completely new business models and revenue streams. In other words, they are moving towards synthesis, where machine is strongly complemented by human expertise. On this basis, new value is generated for their customers, and this new business development may actually result in a significant number of new jobs. In this respect, the companies are specifically attempting to leverage the interdependencies of human and artificial intelligence based on close collaboration between their engineering and machine learning experts.

Complementarity of human and artificial intelligence

The synthesis perspective underscores the importance of complementarity between AI and HI because it involves a high level of both types of intelligence. Nonetheless, any situation with at least a moderate level of HI and AI requires some level of collaboration between AI and HI. Even if companies attempt to modularize the different tasks that need to be performed as much as possible, there will be several important interfaces of HI and AI in these situations. The distinction of pooled, sequential, and reciprocal interdependence of HI and AI provides a helpful starting point for managing the interfaces of the different types of intelligence. In particular, HI may contribute to strengthening a firm's AI applications. At the same time, AI may contribute to enhancing the HI of a firm's employees. Consequently, there may be mutual relationships and a close collaboration between AI and HI, as H. James Wilson and Paul R. Daugherty discuss in their 2018 article entitled 'Humans and AI are joining forces'.[11] According to their argument, a company's employees have three important roles in further strengthening a firm's AI applications.

First, employees need to train AI, for example with regard to machine learning. Here, HI is needed to show the algorithms how a particular work needs to be performed, usually based on large amounts of training data. For example, countless training calls were needed to enable Google's Duplex technology to provide the personal digital assistant with an outstanding ability to conduct phone calls, for example to schedule appointments or make reservations. This training role of humans will continue to be important even if the particular focus of training AI may shift in the future. Currently, firms are exploring in trainings whether personal digital assistants may learn some level of interpersonal intelligence to allow for emotionally appropriate responses in their interactions with humans. Multiple rounds of training are essential to enable significant advances of the assistants in this dimension.

Second, a company's employees are needed to explain the results of processes that are based on AI. Increasingly, AI activities represent something of a black-box procedure, which comes to interesting conclusions, but requires additional expertise to understand how these conclusions were drawn. For example, in the field of medical AI applications, it may be critical to know how the AI weighs multiple input factors to arrive at particular recommendations. In addition, it may be essential to consult human experts which additional steps may be necessary in light of the results of analyses that are based on AI. Here, the changing role of radiologists, which has been discussed earlier in this chapter, provides a good example. While the contribution of HI may change in the context of a growing role of AI, human input may still be critical in the foreseeable future although its particular focus may shift from performing a specific task to explaining the results of an AI performing this task.

Third, human experts may be needed in order to sustain the smooth application of AI. In particular, human experts are needed to check that the AI applications work properly and safely. Accordingly, human intelligence is not only critical in selecting the specific application of AI in the first place, but also in the continuous operation and improvement throughout the everyday use. Here, safety issues may play an important role, for example in the interaction of humans and robots in manufacturing processes. In addition, ethical issues may play a role, as well as data protection and privacy issues, which are particularly relevant in all customer-related interactions. A more detailed discussion of these three roles of human experts in strengthening AI applications may be found in the article by H. James Wilson and Paul R. Daugherty.[12] These three roles are important in many interplays of HI and AI, and they are particularly relevant in the synthesis domain of HI and AI.

Beyond the key role of human experts in strengthening a firm's AI applications, the opposite relationship may be important. This relationship indicates situations where AI augments the abilities and intelligence of human workers. In this regard, AI may also have three key roles in extending human expertise, according to the article 'Humans and AI are joining forces' by H. James Wilson and Paul R. Daugherty.[13] The first way in which AI assists humans refers to situations where AI may amplify HI and human skills. At a very basic level, AI may provide helpful information at the right moment, which enables humans to fully leverage their cognitive abilities. Moreover, particular calculations and analytics may be performed by AI in a more efficient and effective way. Beyond these information handling and data analytics procedures, AI may also help humans to enhance their creativity even if AI is not able to independently provide completely novel and creative solutions. For example, Autodesk has developed the Dreamcatcher AI, which offers designers potentially suitable solutions based on certain criteria that are entered as given. On this basis, designers may focus on assessing the form and function for the particular application.[14]

The second way in which AI may assist humans refers to human-machine interactions. In particular, AI may enable companies to interact with their customers, employees, or third parties much more closely than pure human-to-human interaction would allow. Good examples in this regard are customer service bots or personal digital assistants that are able to handle natural language communication. The percentage of messages or calls that these bots are able to handle autonomously is often above 75 percent, and this percentage is continuously increasing. Consequently, humans may concentrate on a much smaller number of human-to-human communications to solve customer complaints or other situations that the AI may not be able to handle. As such, the AI, especially natural language processing and speech technologies, assists humans in handling massive loads of interaction which could not be performed at the same service level without the use of AI.

The third way in which AI may assist humans refers to embodying the AI in a robot or other machine which may then closely collaborate with human workers. Even if a lot of the public attention concerning AI focuses on robots, AI substantially exceeds the field of robotics. Many AIs, such as Alexa and Siri, are only virtual entities. If it is found to be useful, however, AI can be embodied in some hardware. As such, it may transform a mere hardware product or machine into a smart and at least somewhat intelligent robot. On this basis, there are many emerging opportunities for a closer human-machine collaboration because the AI facilitates a completely different level of smooth, safe, and natural interaction. In particular, AI enables flexible collaboration rather than merely having robots performing well-defined steps and movements. A more thorough discussion of these three ways of AI assisting humans is given in the article by H. James Wilson and Paul R. Daugherty.[15] These three ways are essential in many interplays of HI and AI, and they are particularly relevant in the synthesis domain of HI and AI.

Implications of complementarity

There is no one-type-fits-all relationship between human and artificial intelligence. There is no one answer for all businesses. Rather, all four interplays – Standard, Substitute, Superiority, and Synthesis – will continue to be relevant, to varying degrees, to most large companies. So how should executives respond? Will companies focusing on AI as a substitute for HI have to redirect their initiatives? Probably not – rather, they will need to extend and complement their ongoing AI activities with new approaches that broaden and deepen the relationship between human and artificial intelligence. Failing to investigate this synthesis will lead to opportunities being missed. Three steps are helpful in shaping comprehensive AI activities and creating a program that goes beyond merely pursuing artificial substitutes for human workers to leverage the value creation potential of the synthesis between human and artificial intelligence.

First, executives should continue to pursue substitution and capture efficiency gains based on replacing HI by AI where appropriate. These activities may be considered the baseline of applying AI in order to strengthen the existing business. Often, these efficiency gains may be realized quite quickly after AI applications are implemented. Second, executives need to acknowledge singularity and identify the core strengths of human intelligence in their future businesses. These analyses will be key to achieving a sustainable competitive advantage in digital competitive environments in the future. For the foreseeable future, there will be some key fields, where leading human expertise will provide the basis for competitive advantage despite the substantial advances in AI technology. Third, executives need to go beyond the standard, substitute, and singularity perspectives in order to explore systematically the strategy space that is associated with the synthesis of HI and AI. Without considering the ample opportunities that derive from systematically combining HI and AI, the potential benefits of AI initiatives will only pay off to a very limited degree.

There are many different ways in which a close collaboration and combination of HI and AI may enhance a firm's competitive position and performance. For example, combining the creative intelligence of human employees with the latest machine learning applications may further enhance industrial design and engineering processes. Moreover, combining the interpersonal intelligence of employees with advanced planning and optimization procedures based on AI offers new opportunities for a personalized customer experience. In addition, the combination of machine learning with human decision-making enables more effective and more efficient decisions, for example in approving or blocking credit card transactions. While many of these benefits of closely combining HI and AI derive from efficiency gains, they are also critical in enabling completely new solutions and business models.

With regard to the long-term competitive impact of AI, the largest benefits will most likely derive from a complementary synthesis of human and artificial intelligence that enables completely new ways of creating value. Besides providing the basis for new customer solutions and business models, this synthesis will generate new jobs and fundamentally reshape many existing jobs. Consistent with these arguments, several recent studies suggest that a majority of executives expect a somewhat limited number of jobs to be lost as a result of AI in their companies. Thus, a substantial number of jobs will be lost in many companies, but simultaneously many new jobs will be created. However, an even higher number of jobs will undergo a considerable transformation, requiring employees to change their roles, competencies, and focus in everyday work. In this regard, a key challenge for executives is a proficient orchestration of the transformation processes needed to support both independent and integrated contributions of human and artificial intelligence.

 Chapter 6

Renewing and recombining human and artificial intelligence

Over the past years, there have been broad public discussions about the need to undertake digital transformation processes in virtually all industries. In the context of these discussions about digital transformation and AI, there has been a lot of hype about smart and connected products. This substantial public attention is well deserved, but are these smart and connected products actually 'smart'? Yes, they are – to some degree. However, many of these products are not 'intelligent' enough in light of current discussions about AI with particular emphasis on advanced data analytics and intelligent algorithms. To what degree AI may actually replace and extend HI is not determined by smart and connected products alone. By the same token, robots are only a minor part of AI applications. Rather, we are currently experiencing a new wave of transformation that goes beyond what has been termed 'digital transformation' so far, even if the initial wave of digital transformation is far from over.[1]

From digital transformation to intelligence transformation

In the vast majority of sectors, there is a strong tendency towards a next stage of transformation, which goes beyond the typical evolutions of digital transformation that we have experienced so far. In essence, this next level of disruption is based on a more ample use of AI, and it may be considered a logical next step of the strategic adaptation processes. Therefore, it may be termed 'intelligence transformation'. In this next level of change, a key focus is on fully leveraging the data of smart and connected products by means of intelligent algorithms and advanced analytics – because this usually could not be accomplished by HI. Smart products typically include sensors to enable real-time data monitoring, such as the sensor of a car's anti-lock braking system. On this basis, a connectivity component allows for interacting with the Internet and with other products. An example here are the protocols for connectivity in the case of autonomous driving. These smart and connected products have been a major step, and many more of these products will be needed in the years to come.[2]

However, smart and connected products only provide the basis for a more extensive use of AI, for example advanced algorithms that actually allow for safe autonomous driving. Consequently, the digital transformation initiatives that have been started in most established companies in the past years are only necessary, but not sufficient for arriving at intelligent new solutions for the digital future. As a consequence of digitalization initiatives, many companies now collect large volumes of data. Some of this data is more technology-related, for example about internal machinery and production processes. Other data is more market-related, for instance about interactions with customers at multiple touchpoints throughout the customer journey.

On this basis, executives and operational managers face the challenge of exploiting the value of these enormous volumes of data – and so far, many firms and individual experts have not yet succeeded in these complex tasks. There is often substantial value in leveraging the insights from a variety of data sources. One major advantage is the dramatic reduction of operational costs for predicting future events, for example enabling preventive maintenance in internal operations as well as more specific interactions and targeted offers to individual customers in order to keep high levels of customer satisfaction. While these potential benefits are relatively clear on paper, they are often hard to realize in firms' everyday activities. Data from digitalization initiatives is nice to have, but the data alone is often not enough for fully leveraging the opportunities of digital transformation. So where do we go from here?

There are multiple reasons for many companies' problems in profiting from their digitalization initiatives in general and in capturing the value of their data in particular. Some of these problems boil down to a limited effectiveness and efficiency in implementing the digitalization programs. For example, many firms experience major difficulties in designing new business models for their digital solutions and services. In addition, many companies pursue a variety of isolated digital projects, but lack a systematic strategic approach to cover the full strategy space for digital transformation. Another typical problem is the management and direction of the portfolio of digital projects, which often have multiple interdependencies and which tend to complement one another. These typical implementation barriers can often be overcome by means of a proficient management of the digitalization initiatives.

However, the effective management of a firm's digital transformation initiatives is often only part of a more complex story. In this regard, there are more fundamental problems in capturing the value from data, which go beyond typical implementation challenges. In fact, most experts emphasize the value of data when discussing the benefits of digital transformation for firms from many different sectors. Nonetheless, the value of data per se is usually relatively limited. Data is only the beginning, and in most cases multiple data sources need to be combined to generate meaningful information. This step from data to information is managed successfully in many companies. To actually achieve new revenue streams from external partners or efficiency increases in internal processes, however, the information further needs to be transformed into knowledge and intelligence.

The knowledge and intelligence are typically the sources of value from data and the basis of competitive advantages in a digital future. At the same time, this knowledge and intelligence are often a principal reason for the limited success rates of digitalization initiatives. While many of these initiatives have led to some promising results, they often have not lived up to the initial expectations of the firms' executives. Beyond implementation difficulties, the challenges of generating and exploiting meaningful knowledge and intelligence from the underlying data and information are one of the major root causes for a more intense use of AI in many firms. These companies have realized that advanced analytics and intelligent algorithms are key ingredients to turning their digitalization programs into successful initiatives with a clear positive impact in terms of market position, competitive advantage, and financial return for the organization.

Without relying on big data analyses, advanced analytics, and various other mechanisms, it will be difficult to fully reap the advantages of the substantial investments in digital transformation. Drawing exclusively on the HI of internal experts will often not be enough in light of the high complexity of the digitalization initiatives, especially in established companies. Human experts are still very much needed, and they have a key role in benefiting from the vast volumes of data and information that are generated in many firms' digitalization initiatives. Nonetheless, these human experts are usually unable to cope with all data and analyses based on established technologies. Therefore, they increasingly rely on the latest AI technology for replacing or at least for complementing their own analyses.

In this respect, many large firms, such as Apple, Bank of America, and General Electric, have intensified their use of AI technology in recent years. Typically, the focus of these activities is on realizing efficiency benefits by replacing human labor with intelligent algorithms. This approach often allows for a relatively independent management of AI and HI. In these cases, the different types of intelligence can be developed in relative isolation. For example, firms may enhance their expertise in particular fields of data analytics and in addition hire new engineers for specific technology fields to strengthen their human expertise. However, a growing number of companies go a step further, and they attempt to achieve new growth opportunities by complementing the two types of intelligence.

Under these conditions, the two types of intelligence are not applied independently anymore, but they strengthen one another. This strategic approach goes beyond the independent management of multiple types of intelligence. As such, it often leads to completely new solutions and business models, which include intelligent algorithms based on data from smart and connected products. Thus, this approach particularly enables new ways of generating innovation and growth beyond increasing efficiency and optimization. Independent of a firm's emphasis on enhancing efficiency or growth, however, the growing use of AI calls for clear strategic direction in the new wave of intelligence transformation rather than digital transformation.

Intelligence renewal and recombination

Many companies not only need to enhance their levels of AI while continuing to develop their HI. Rather, they additionally need a meta-intelligence as a higher-order intelligence for transforming the different types of HI and AI in line with corporate strategy and business strategies. This dynamic transformation over time will not be achieved by relying only on human and artificial intelligence. Rather, it requires a meta-intelligence for transforming, upgrading, augmenting, and innovating the intelligence types. Consequently, the firms need Intelligence^X – comprising the different types of AI, HI, and meta-intelligence. Specifically, this meta-intelligence involves the renewal and recombination of the distinct types of intelligence, which is comparable to the intertemporal evolution of organizational capabilities and innovation processes.[3]

The renewal of the two intelligence types may be needed due to advances in AI technology or the need for deepening and extending a firm's HI to new fields. Consequently, one type or both types of intelligence are enhanced and upgraded. Thus, a firm's intelligence is renewed because new components are added to the existing intelligence, potentially replacing some existing components. Beyond renewal, the recombination of the two intelligence types may be necessary because of positive or negative interdependencies among them. These interdependencies may call for adapting a firm's intelligence architecture, which describes the interplay of AI and HI. In the case of pure reconfiguration, the intelligence types are not renewed. Instead, their connections and interrelationships are changed and enhanced.

Depending on the extent of renewal and recombination, there are different transformations, which are consistent with extant insights into transforming innovation activities and product features. Depending on the particular situation and need for change, companies may rely on the independent renewal or recombination of their two types of intelligence. In addition, firms may simultaneously pursue both renewal and recombination to some degree. This leads to the following four transformations, which are illustrated in Figure 4: incremental, modular, architectural, and radical transformation. First, incremental transformation involves only a limited renewal and recombination of AI and HI. Examples are updates of AI technology to enable new functionalities or the selective implementation of a new creativity technique in order to better leverage human idea generation and intelligence. Both of these approaches could recently

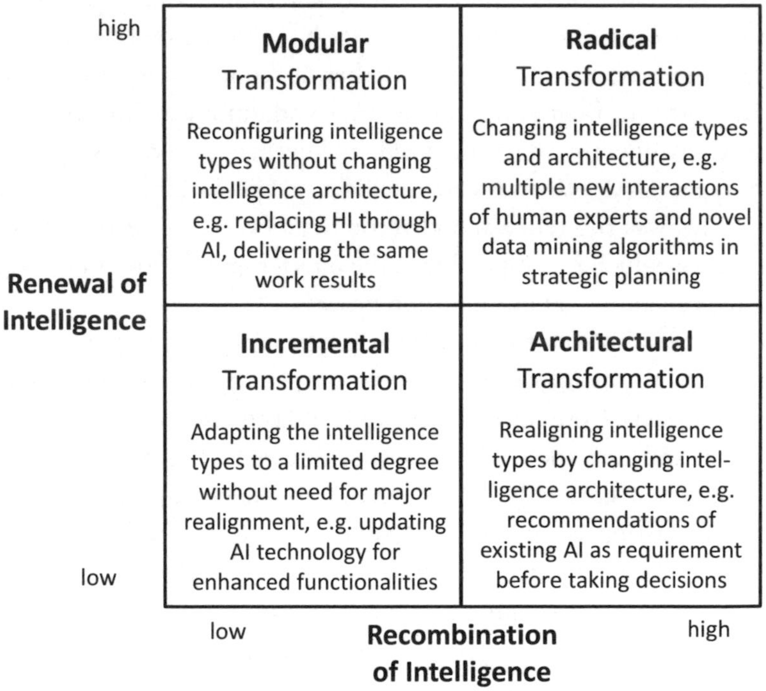

	Recombination of Intelligence	
Renewal of Intelligence high	**Modular Transformation** Reconfiguring intelligence types without changing intelligence architecture, e.g. replacing HI through AI, delivering the same work results	**Radical Transformation** Changing intelligence types and architecture, e.g. multiple new interactions of human experts and novel data mining algorithms in strategic planning
low	**Incremental Transformation** Adapting the intelligence types to a limited degree without need for major realignment, e.g. updating AI technology for enhanced functionalities	**Architectural Transformation** Realigning intelligence types by changing intelligence architecture, e.g. recommendations of existing AI as requirement before taking decisions
	low Recombination of Intelligence high	

Figure 4: Transformations of intelligence
(Source: Lichtenthaler, 2019, Journal of Business Strategy[4])

be observed in many large companies as diverse as Facebook and Harley-Davidson.

Second, modular transformation includes a significant renewal of intelligence, whereas the level of recombination is relatively limited. Thus, the intelligence architecture is largely untouched, but the individual intelligence types are substantially reconfigured.[5] With regard to HI, for example, many companies, such as Apple and the German software company SAP, have strongly transformed their human-based innovation processes to focus on design thinking logic in addition to traditional innovation processes. This has often occurred quite independently from AI activities, and the overall intelligence architecture has only been affected to a limited degree. With regard to AI, this modular transformation also involves the substitution of one type of intelligence by the other. Accordingly, modular transformation is also the transformation that has received most public attention in recent years because many firms' strategic initiatives have focused on replacing HI by means of AI, which would deliver nearly identical work results. Consequently, the interdependencies of the two types of intelligence have not changed substantially because the focus is on enhancing efficiency by getting similar results at lower cost.

Third, architectural transformation focuses on the recombination of the two types of intelligence, whereas the level of renewal is limited.[6] This transformation has hitherto often been overlooked because most companies do not yet take an integrative perspective on their different types of intelligence. They rather have started somewhat isolated AI initiatives, and they continue to nurture the HI of their experts. In contrast, a systematic understanding of the interplay of the intelligence types in terms of an intelligence architecture has largely been neglected – let alone a targeted realignment of the intelligence types over time. An example is an update of a company's investment guidelines in order to make the consultation of existing AI a requirement before taking decisions. This is what the investment management firms WorldQuant and Aspect Capital have done. Accordingly, the focus of architectural transformation is not on implementing completely new technology. Rather, the focus is on revising the interdependencies of AI and HI, thus changing the connections of technology that was already used at least in some parts of the company.

Fourth, radical transformation involves high levels of both renewal and recombination. Consequently, a company's intelligence is updated and enhanced, while simultaneously changing the intelligence architecture. An example here is the implementation of new and advanced data mining algorithms in a company's strategic planning processes, which would involve a close interaction with the HI of the strategy department. Consequently, there are many new interdependencies of HI with new AI technology, which requires a substantial adaptation of a firm's intelligence architecture. Another example are start-up companies like Talenya, which use advanced data analytics to fill roles and to pre-select candidates for job vacancies with their customers. The new technology determines whether candidates are invited to a personal interview, and the final decision is based on the scoring of AI and experts from the HR department.

Transformation steps

The wave of digital transformation with smart and connected products is not yet over, and the wave of fully implementing AI is far from reaching its inflection point. Consequently, we have seen only a marginal impact of transforming a firm's different types of intelligence. Most probably, proficiently managing the interdependencies of human and artificial intelligence will become a key part of firms' transformation initiatives over the next years. Here, a meta-intelligence, which contributes to steering the evolution of the two types of intelligence, will be critical. The more executives attempt to leverage the combinative effects of the two types of intelligence rather than merely replacing one by the other, the more important the meta-intelligence will be.

Without this meta-intelligence, most AI initiatives will be isolated endeavors, which may have positive effects but likely will not live up to the expectations. Of course, firms without a well-developed meta-intelligence may also rely on new technology, and they may do this quite successfully. In a similar vein, firms without a strong meta-intelligence may develop the competencies of their human experts to cover new fields of technology and expertise. In light of the growing importance of AI, however, companies with a limited meta-intelligence will have a hard time leveraging the benefits of their different types of intelligence. These companies may manage their existing intelligence types in the right way. Most probably, however, they will not develop the right intelligence types over time.

When companies lack a strong meta-intelligence, the following and many more tasks may not be accomplished proficiently: asking the right questions for further developing a firm's intelligence architecture, deciding about the use of artificial or human intelligence and skills, ensuring high usability of AI for the particular applications in the organization, initiating change processes to encourage open attitudes towards interacting with AI, adapting the intelligence architecture to incorporate new skills and expertise, managing interdependencies and potential conflicts between various types of intelligence. These tasks are key ingredients of a meta-intelligence, which enables companies to successfully pursue incremental, modular, architectural, or radical transformations of their intelligence types. Rather than undertaking these transformations in an isolated way, the meta-intelligence allows for a high level of alignment with a firm's current situation and managerial challenges. So how should executives respond?

First, top managers have to acknowledge the need for fully leveraging the benefits of transforming their companies towards AI. There will hardly be an alternative to this transformation in the long term. While many companies in general and top executives in particular are open to adapting most recent technology, many other organizations are very reluctant in this regard. Often, the executives in these companies are satisfied with having started some digital transformation initiatives, and they want to go no further until the expected benefits of these initiatives materialize. While this reluctance may be a natural move to some degree, it does not take into account the fact that the full benefits of digital transformation will often depend on a proficient use of advanced technology in order to leverage and to monetize the data that is generated in digital transformation initiatives.

Second, executives have to exploit the benefits of complementing the different types of intelligence rather than merely substituting HI by AI. A mere substitution of one intelligence type by the other may constitute an important strategic move for a company. However, many benefits of a stronger use of AI will be unrealized unless the interdependencies of the two intelligence types are considered. Because of emphasizing the independent use of the intelligence types, most firms' AI initiatives have so far focused on incremental and modular transformation, which provide the basis for a relatively isolated application of advanced analytics and complex data mining algorithms. In contrast, the opportunities of architectural and radical transformation have gone unnoticed, but these transformations are essential for capturing the benefits of complementing the two types of intelligence.

Third, firms need to develop a meta-intelligence for successfully managing their transformation in terms of renewing and recombining human and artificial intelligence. Merely focusing on each type of intelligence will likely not be enough for gaining a competitive advantage in the future. In particular, the meta-intelligence goes along with a systematic understanding of the firm's intelligence architecture and its dynamic adaptation over time. Often, this will require substantial cross-functional collaboration as well as the development of new competencies in particular departments. For example, HR departments may need to develop at least sufficient knowledge about the opportunities and challenges of applying particular data-related technologies. Only with this prior knowledge may HR experts successfully collaborate with the in-house experts in AI, digitalization, and information technology to optimally design future job profiles in interaction with AI.

Fourth, executives need to balance their companies' focus on efficiency benefits from AI with sufficient attention to innovation and growth. A systematic analysis of the benefits of transforming the two types of intelligence will enable firms to leave their comfort zones of using advanced analytics and related technologies for cost reduction and optimization purposes. Beyond leading to completely new solutions, which enable new business models and revenue streams, the four transformations will strengthen a firm's flexibility based on a superior design of the intelligence architecture. Efficiency and optimization are core features of intelligence transformations, and many of these cost-related benefits may be achieved in shorter periods relative to innovation-related opportunities. However, an exclusive focus on these cost-related advantages will place close constraints on the potential benefits of intelligence transformations.

Fifth, companies need to start exploring the broader perspective of the four transformations now. There is some truth in the argument that orchestrating the perfect interplay of AI and HI for the future may not be possible today. One major reason for this argument is the foreseeable further evolution of intelligent algorithms and data analytics in the next years. Therefore, technological solutions that are implemented today may well have to be substantially adapted in a few years. Nonetheless, companies need to get going now. Without enhancing their competence levels in managing intelligence transformation beyond mere technology challenges, any intelligence-based competitive advantage will be difficult in the future. Sticking to the comfort zone of limited applications of AI without attention to the overall intelligence architecture is not enough, even if the companies concerned were open to broader changes in the future. A period of experimentation is necessary to achieve an intelligence-based competitive advantage, and companies need to start experimenting now.

The impact of AI has only just begun to unfold in most companies. With further advances in different technology fields, the application opportunities will continue to grow, but many firms are not well-prepared for leveraging these technological evolutions. Hiring a few AI experts and implementing specific solutions may allow for replacing some HI by means of intelligent algorithms. These managerial moves will often enable cost savings, which can be achieved in relatively short periods. However, the full impact of AI will go considerably beyond this independent exploitation of advanced data analytics and intelligent algorithms. It will strongly affect the entire intelligence architecture of companies, with a substantial impact on the activities of human experts. While some companies are relatively open to proactively pursuing the transformation of their intelligence architectures, many others are reluctant to do so on account of corporate cultures that are not conducive to major organizational changes.

To overcome these barriers to change and to fully leverage the potential benefits, companies need a new type of intelligence beyond AI and HI. This meta-intelligence is directed at transforming an organization's intelligence architecture in line with corporate strategy by renewing and recombining the different types of intelligence. Thus, it is a higher-order intelligence because merely addressing the two intelligence types in isolation is not enough. Rather, companies will increasingly need Intelligence^X – comprising AI, human intelligence, and meta-intelligence. Future competitive advantages may derive from a particular strength in any of these three types of intelligence. As such, companies may outperform competitors with similar levels of the two intelligence types due to a higher level of meta-intelligence. Like AI and HI, the meta-intelligence is driven by nature and nurture – and executives need to start now to develop this third type of intelligence as a basis for Intelligence^X in their future organizations.

Part C
Strategy

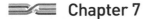 Chapter 7

Business innovation and evolutionary fitness

The challenges of AI and digitalization continue to be at the top of the strategic agendas of most large and medium-sized companies. As a result of the considerable managerial challenges, many companies' digitalization initiatives have failed to live up to the expectations. These limited success rates constitute a major strategic problem for many senior managers, whose companies face the dilemma of present success in their established businesses – while foreseeing a weak future position in AI and digital businesses. The different technology trends, market applications, and management challenges of digitalization and AI are already having a disruptive impact within many industries. In fact, this evolution leads to blurring industry boundaries and to the emergence of new competitors for many established companies. As such, executives expect a major wave of transformation for a variety of industries, including automotive, chemicals, electronics, machinery, and information technology. By now, many large and medium-sized companies have acknowledged the need to respond to and to influence the disruptive evolutions that may change the very core of their businesses.

Accordingly, many firms have formulated detailed digital strategies, and they have assigned a Chief Digital Officer, who is responsible for digital transformation and product-related AI implementation. On this basis, many companies have launched corporate digitalization initiatives and AI programs. At the core of these programs are usually transformation activities in order to prepare a company for the digital future. This is a clear strength of these initiatives because transformation is essential for successfully coping with the substantial changes in the industry and business environment. More specifically, many companies' digitalization and

AI initiatives concentrate on purely digital innovation. While this is partly necessary, an exclusive focus on AI and digital innovation will most likely be insufficient – and potentially detrimental. In fact, it may limit a company's ability to adapt to the challenges of intelligence-based competitive environments. As such, a pure focus on AI with insufficient non-digital innovation is actually a severe weakness of the AI initiatives of many companies. In particular, implementing AI based on established business models will often perpetuate a company's dominant managerial logic – and this logic may be a powerful barrier to sustaining today's competitive advantage and to achieving a strong competitive position in the digital future.[1]

Digital and non-digital innovation

Digital innovation involves AI and all other uses of digital technology in a business, including embedded sensors, mobile solutions, connectivity, and cloud solutions. These technologies help to enhance a company's manufacturing as well as other business processes, and they provide the basis for new applications. However, to actually arrive at completely new product features which enable new solutions, further innovation activities may be required, and these activities will often not be digital. In turn, they are not 'old school' analog innovations, but rather critical strategic moves of innovation and corporate entrepreneurship that allow for fully leveraging the potential of AI and digital technology. Examples are new services that enable companies to offer integrated solutions that comprise physical products along with intangible digital services. Other examples are new business models that help companies monetize their new digital market applications. Only the combination of AI and other technology-based digital innovations with non-digital innovations will make the new applications a market success.

This need for combining digital and non-digital innovation is best illustrated with some examples. Chemical companies, such as Dow Chemical, may use AI for advanced big data analytics to identify cross-selling opportunities drawing on a clearer understanding of their customers' needs and processes. A pure focus on this digital innovation, however, would prevent the firms from using data about the customers of their customers at the very end of the value chain. This data may allow for gaining new insights into final market applications as a basis for non-digital innovation in order to enhance the chemicals and to better serve the final market needs. In a similar vein, financial services companies, such as Deutsche Bank, may strengthen their transaction efficiency by means of AI and other digital technologies. At the same time, an exclusive focus on these new technologies will limit their ability to identify new growth opportunities based on applying new business models for fully utilizing the existing resources.

Moreover, a manufacturer of hearing aids, such as Sivantos with its Signia brand, may use AI and other digital technologies to enhance customers' experience of its products, e. g. based on an intelligent smartphone app with multiple functions, including basic functionalities, such as indicating the battery status for the hearing aids. This digital innovation focusing on connectivity solutions is an important step, but it would actually limit the innovation activities to hearing aids. Consequently, the company would be vulnerable to new competitors that offer hearables with a variety of functions, such as phone calls, playing music, or ambient assisted living functions based on AI. Without offering these additional functionalities, which require non-digital innovations, traditional hearing aid manufacturers will likely face severe competitive difficulties in the future.

How do established companies score in terms of digital and non-digital innovation? Based on a variety of company examples as well as prior studies,[2] four observations are particularly noteworthy, depending on varying degrees of digital and non-digital innovation from incremental improvements to radical novelties. First, many companies and executives still stick to their traditional dominant logics because their businesses continue to be relatively strong and they do not yet see the need to respond actively (Figure 5). However, this reluctance will most likely lead to severe competitive challenges in the medium term. Some companies specifically attempt to avoid these limitations by questioning established assumptions in their core business. For example, Unilever attempts to reimagine how to connect with consumers across key digital touch-points on the path to purchase in a data-driven ecosystem.[3]

Second, many companies have established systematic innovation management, corporate entrepreneurship, strategic agility, and lean startup programs over the past decades. These activities comprise product innovation, process innovation, and services innovation, and they have proved very helpful in the past. Nonetheless, these systematic innovation processes are usually insufficient for digital innovations, and they do not sufficiently consider the new management challenges of digitalization.

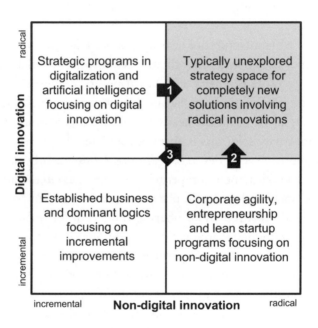

Figure 5: Digital and non-digital innovation

Third, many companies have realized the limitations of their traditional innovation activities, and they have started particular AI and digitalization programs. However, these initiatives typically focus exclusively on digital innovation and AI. For example, the companies optimize their internal manufacturing processes based on new digital solutions and advanced analytics. Moreover, they enhance further business processes based on Internet of Things solutions and enhanced analytics. Digital businesses need to make sense of their data assets, and this can only be achieved with innovative AI applications[4]. Due to the typical focus on strengthening efficiency, however, many companies neglect to fully exploit the opportunities of digitalization. Mark Bernstein, former President of Xerox PARC, explains: "Companies need to balance the use of digital technologies to enhance internal efficiencies with the creation of completely new digital solutions that will drive innovation and spark growth."[5]

Fourth, these companies particularly neglect the opportunities that would result from combining and bundling digital innovation with non-digital innovation. Capturing the benefits of this complementary role of the different innovation types would help the companies to go beyond efficiency gains and to profit from effectiveness increases. In particular, the combination of digital and non-digital innovation would enable the firms to develop completely new solutions and integrated service offerings comprising digital products, services, and processes. For instance, the German sportswear manufacturer Adidas challenges conventions with its Speedfactory, which combines multiple technologies including 3D printing to arrive at completely novel solutions.[6] However, these huge opportunities are neglected in the large majority of companies in the automotive, chemical, electronics, and machinery sectors due to the optimization focus of their digitalization initiatives. Consequently, the opportunities for new entrants to disrupt established businesses in mature industries continue.

So how can executives overcome the limitations of most firms' strategic focus with respect to AI? Beyond the relatively static recommendations that have been given in many earlier studies,[7] three strategic moves are particularly noteworthy from a dynamic perspective, which considers the adaptation of ongoing strategic initiatives over time. The strategic move 'new revenue streams' is indicated by arrow 1 in Figure 5, and it describes the strategic extension of ongoing AI programs beyond efficiency gains for today's core business. Drawing on available technology, many of these programs can be easily extended in order to generate completely new revenue streams based on innovative business models. Arrow 2 in Figure 5 refers to 'new digital opportunities', and it describes the transformation of innovation programs to address digital market opportunities related to AI. For example, this may involve defining a threshold level of at least 50 percent of all innovation projects or all innovation expenditures referring to AI and digital projects. Consequently, the portfolio management of innovation projects may have to be changed substantially to incorporate this intelligence-based goal. Finally, arrow 3 in Figure 5 refers to 'new strategic programs' and indicates the start of completely new strategic initiatives in addition to existing innovation and AI programs. These new initiatives may specifically target highly innovative concepts with a high degree of AI for new markets.

A convincing strategic initiative for overcoming the limitations of many firms' current activities should consider the following steps to go beyond the mere optimization of existing processes. AI and digitalization involve new technology, but companies usually need to start with a strategic analysis of the impact of the digital technologies on their business models. On this basis, opportunities for strengthening efficiency and for developing completely new solutions with enhanced customer benefits on the markets are considered. Then, appropriate new business models and suitable bundles of digital and non-digital innovations for integrated solutions based on AI can be developed. The digital implementation of these innovations based on new AI solutions, often together with external technology suppliers, is an important next step. Finally, the market launch of the new solutions draws on AI and further considers the new business models and potential other non-digital innovations. Consequently, it goes substantially beyond the mere implementation of AI applications, and it involves other non-digital innovations.

Technical and evolutionary fitness

Companies undertake AI efforts to achieve outputs with respect to each type of intelligence and meta-intelligence. The distinction between effort and output is important because these two aspects differ substantially. An efficiency factor[8] between a firm's effort and output in AI indicates that companies vary in their ability to benefit from their AI efforts. The efficiency factor indicates that AI efforts do not automatically result in AI outputs, especially with respect to the high failure rates in profiting from AI. Moreover, it underscores that companies may strongly differ in their AI outputs despite similar efforts and vice versa because of differences in implementation. There are strong differences in companies' efficiency of transforming AI effort into superior output in terms of financial performance. Some companies have a limited output despite major investments because of relatively low AI implementation or inappropriate business models. In addition, AI output merely provides the foundation for achieving superior outcomes, but it does not automatically strengthen a company's performance.[9]

In this regard, AI is a major source of performance increases because it enables companies to avoid competing exclusively on a cost basis, especially if AI is combined with other non-digital innovations. However, profiting from AI requires efficiency increases or innovation outputs rather than mere AI efforts, which primarily entail costs in the short run. This distinction highlights the need for differentiating between short-term and long-term performance effects of AI. Businesses with a low efficiency factor in implementing AI may be unable to benefit from AI because their outputs require excessive efforts. Businesses with high efficiency factors, by contrast, may achieve superior performance over considerable time by leveraging their different types of intelligence. The meta-intelligence even allows companies to sustain superior performance over a long or even unlimited time because it enables them to transform their intelligence architectures to continuously achieve suitable intelligence levels. Jointly, the different types of intelligence provide the basis for sustainable superior performance.

This logic helps to disentangle a somewhat complex relationship between AI and performance. Specifically, an intelligence-based view suggests that companies invest in AI if there are strong links between their AI efforts and outputs as well as strong financial returns to the different types of outputs. Businesses may be unable to achieve value from their intelli gence architecture because of difficulties in transforming efforts into outputs or because of difficulties in transforming outputs into superior performance. These companies will either limit their AI efforts, or they need to find ways to strengthen their effort-output link in AI or the AI-performance link. This discussion underscores the need for a meta-intelligence and for an intertemporal perspective on designing a firm's intelligence architecture. Moreover, the distinction of AI efforts, outputs, and company performance helps to incorporate distinct views on the causality of the AI-performance relationship.[10] Businesses invest in AI efforts if they expect a sufficient return on these efforts in terms of outputs and performance. At the same time, a company's AI efforts influence its future outputs and performance. In this respect, a meta-intelligence is critical because it enables companies to renew their intelligence architecture and to increase the likelihood of positive performance effects of the different types of intelligence.

These arguments are related to the distinction of technical fitness and evolutionary fitness in the strategic management literature. Specifically, technical fitness describes how effectively a particular type of intelligence performs its intended function when divided by its cost.[11] Accordingly, an intelligence's technical fitness indicates a company's productivity in nurturing and utilizing this intelligence because higher quality levels do not automatically entail higher costs and vice versa. Therefore, it is helpful to consider technical fitness rather than exclusively considering a company's quality or cost in AI activities. However, technical fitness alone is only necessary, but not sufficient for achieving high levels of financial performance. In particular, companies additionally need evolutionary fitness for their different types of intelligence. Evolutionary fitness describes how well a particular type of intelligence enables a company to strengthen its financial performance by augmenting or transforming its intelligence architecture.[12]

For example, a specific intelligence, such as the creative intelligence of human experts, may have a high evolutionary fitness despite low technical fitness if the competitive conditions in the environment are favorable. Nonetheless, companies cannot easily strengthen the evolutionary fitness of all types of intelligence because resources and budget are limited, while they face severe competitive constraints in the shape of established companies and potential new entrants that also aim at leveraging their intelligence architectures. Rather, firms need to balance their AI activities in multiple ways. Besides balancing the use of AI and HI, they need to balance the different types of intelligence and meta-intelligence. A repeated utilization of a particular type of AI or HI, e.g. interpersonal intelligence, may enhance a company's efficiency in performing this type of intelligence. At the same time, it may complicate even minor changes of this type based on the meta-intelligence.[13] In contrast, if a company repeatedly pursues the renewal and recombination of its intelligence architecture, it reduces the risks of lock-in effects if environmental changes require a revised intelligence. However, a regular transformation of the different types of intelligence may hinder businesses in achieving the maximum output of these intelligences. Thus, companies face a major trade-off between using AI, HI, and meta-intelligence, which calls for balancing these intelligences in alignment with their strategies.

Intelligence and meta-intelligence

The discussion of combining AI with other non-digital innovations highlights the need for thinking beyond efficiency increases by means of implementing relatively isolated AI applications. While this topic underscores the complementarity of multiple types of intelligence, the distinction of technical and evolutionary fitness further highlights the role of the meta-intelligence. The meta-intelligence dynamically adapts and transforms a company's intelligence architecture over time. Thus, it is essential for further developing the different types of HI and AI in light of changes in a firm's competitive environment. Besides enhancing the technical fitness of these different intelligence types, the meta-intelligence is critical for strengthening the evolutionary fitness of the intelligence types. Thus, the meta-intelligence is also critical for managing the trade-offs between the different types of intelligence as well as the trade-offs between utilizing and strengthening the intelligence types or renewing and recombining them with the meta-intelligence.

Accordingly, meta-intelligence refers to a second-order intelligence, which dynamically transforms the different types of HI and AI. An overemphasis on using meta-intelligence will most probably result in negative performance consequences because it limits a company's possibilities to develop high levels of proficiency in the specific types of HI and AI. In contrast to meta-intelligence, these intelligence types may be regarded as regular or first-order intelligences. Since meta-intelligence refers to the dynamic renewal and recombination of the different types of AI and HI, it represents the characteristics of a second-order intelligence. Only by performing these higher-level activities of renewal and recombination, can a company ensure that its intelligence architecture remains up to date. For example, human expertise and AI may be upgraded by means of hiring new experts or implementing new algorithms.

In this respect, there are important differences between HI and AI on the one hand and meta-intelligence on the other. For example, the different types of first-order intelligence primarily rely on the individual learning of human experts or on the machine learning of AI. In contrast, the meta-intelligence primarily draws on organizational learning of the entire company as well as so-called second-order learning, which helps the firm to adapt its different types of HI and AI over time in response to new environmental opportunities and threats. These differences are displayed in Table 2. Specifically, HI and AI may provide a contribution to gaining a competitive advantage at a particular moment. Thus, they typically also have a relatively direct effect on company performance. Contrary to these effects, the meta-intelligence primarily has an indirect performance impact through the renewal and recombination of the different types of HI and AI. On this basis, the meta-intelligence is critical for sustaining a competitive advantage over longer periods.

In the implementation of AI, most executives thoroughly analyze whether the applications actually comprise the latest data analytics solutions and algorithms. In a similar vein, most companies have established systematic processes for continuously developing their human expertise in alignment with corporate strategy. For example, most large companies use

Criteria	Intelligence	Meta-Intelligence
Approach	Human, artificial	Renewal, recombination
Learning	Individual learning, machine learning	Organizational learning, second-order learning
Advantage	Gain a competitive advantage	Sustain a competitive advantage
Impact	Relatively direct performance impact	Relatively indirect performance impact

Table 2: Comparison of intelligence types
(Source: Lichtenthaler, 2019, Next Industry[14])

sophisticated leadership development programs and trainings in order to upgrade and to develop their different types of HI. Moreover, businesses usually design clear competence profiles before hiring new employees. On this basis, they may increase the probability that the new employees bring the expertise, skills, and intelligence that are needed in a digital future. Thus, companies usually have proficient mechanisms for actively managing HI and AI. The recent strategic initiatives for implementing AI in many companies may be considered an indicator of this systematic management approach. Thus, executives are usually aware of the need for managing the distinct types of HI and AI.

In contrast, the need for actively developing the meta-intelligence is often overlooked. Accordingly, most companies do not systematically address the interplay of HI and AI. Moreover, most companies do not proficiently analyze their intelligence architectures to identify any need for transforming or updating them. Thus, the dynamic renewal and recombination of the different types of HI and AI mostly happens randomly, or – if it happens at all – it is only managed unconsciously. The meta-intelligence is particularly important for designing the intelligence architecture in a way that enables positive synergies among the multiple types of intelligence while avoiding negative effects. In turn, these interactions are critical for using AI for innovation beyond mere efficiency increases. Consequently, the limited emphasis on meta-intelligence is among the principal reasons for the unrealized potential that exists in many companies with regard to an integrated intelligence architecture, which would help to leverage the benefits of combining AI and digital innovation with further types of non-digital innovation.

 Chapter 8

Core competencies and competitive advantage

How can a company achieve an intelligence-based competitive advantage? Essentially, this is what strategic management is all about – gaining and sustaining a competitive advantage. If we accept the growing importance of AI as a no-brainer, particular applications of AI should at least provide the basis for achieving a competitive advantage. In addition, HI continues to be relevant, so managers need a clear understanding of how HI provides the basis for achieving a competitive advantage. Furthermore, executives need to leverage the interdependencies of the different types of intelligence in their organization. Moreover, there may be particular benefits of the meta-intelligence. All of these strategic questions are critical if companies aim to exploit the opportunities of the recent advances in AI – and if they do not want to limit their benefits to temporary advances from implementing a few relatively isolated AI applications some months or years before their established competitors do the same.

Despite all the hype about AI in recent years, however, these questions have been largely overlooked in many companies. This is particularly surprising because the application of AI solutions often aims at enhancing the analytical rigor of strategic and operational decisions. Nonetheless, many companies have pursued an ad-hoc approach to setting up and implementing AI initiatives. While this approach has often contributed to the emergence of implementation problems, it has also led to an unclear strategic direction of the AI programs in many companies, not to mention the integration with HI and the role of the meta-intelligence. Thus, many firms do not yet fully profit from their AI initiatives, and it is unlikely that this will change in the future because an unclear strategic direction limits the benefits and the potential returns to the AI investments. To further aggravate this challenging situation, many firms will have a difficult time in identifying the root causes for their managerial difficulties with regard to profiting from AI because many basic strategic questions concerning AI and the intelligence architecture are still open.

However, addressing and convincingly answering these key questions is necessary for identifying potential problems and limited benefits – or ideally setting up a suitable strategy right from the start. Accordingly, it is often helpful to start with these basic strategic questions to at least increase the probability of achieving an intelligence-based competitive advantage. In this regard, it is particularly helpful to consider the entire strategy space – including blue ocean markets and red ocean markets – that would be enabled by AI and integrated intelligence in general. While red oceans refer to established markets with strong competition, blue oceans describe new markets with limited competition.[1] These blue ocean markets may be developed by commercializing completely new solutions based on AI or by closely integrating the AI solutions with HI and meta-intelligence. By systematically addressing blue oceans and red oceans, companies avoid the mistake of limiting their AI strategies to implementing specific solutions for achieving minor advantages in their traditional red ocean markets.

Accordingly, executives need to accept the relevance of pursuing intelligence-based competitive advantages in the future. This understanding implies that a competitive advantage does not necessarily derive from superior AI solutions. Rather, an intelligence-based advantage may also result from higher levels of HI or the meta-intelligence. Companies typically will need some core competencies that involve different types of intelligence. However, not all companies need to become top experts in AI. While most companies will need some internal AI competencies in the future, these competencies may well refer to the application of AI rather than to the development of new AI solutions. In addition, businesses may further focus on the combination of AI with HI and the meta-intelligence.

Thus, there are ample opportunities for realizing a competitive advantage in intelligence-based competition without excelling at developing new algorithms and advanced analytics solutions. Fundamentally, a company's potential core competencies, which are based on some type of intelligence, need to be chosen and developed in alignment with its corporate and business strategies. Accordingly, a company's individual strategic decisions will determine the importance of the different types of intelligence. While there generally is a growing importance of AI – and this evolution will continue for several years – the particular focus and strategic role of AI in a firm's competitive actions strongly depends on the strategic emphasis. Thus, the growing relevance of AI constitutes an additional strategic variable that needs to be considered in executive decisions. As such, it extends a company's strategy space, but it does not automatically require all companies to develop core competencies in AI. Rather, it may well be an appropriate strategy to rely on some standard AI solutions and to connect those solutions in an intelligent way to the other components of a company's intelligence architecture in order to realize new business opportunities. To some extent, these opportunities derive from the markets for intelligence.

Markets for intelligence

There are markets for intelligence, and these markets broaden a firm's strategic options for achieving an intelligence-based competitive advantage. What are these markets for intelligence? Of course, companies cannot simply shop for a particular type of intelligence. The opportunities for acquiring disembodied intelligence are relatively limited. Instead, transactions of intelligence often involve embodied intelligence. For example, HI is embodied in human experts. Thus, companies may hire new employees in order to strengthen particular types of HI, such as creative or interpersonal intelligence. In a similar vein, AI is often embodied in products, services, components, or software solutions. Thus, companies may purchase robots and software to strengthen particular types of AI, such as specific algorithms based on machine learning and robotics applications. Transactions involving these embodied types of intelligence are relatively common.

By contrast, transactions of disembodied intelligence are relatively uncommon – at least depending on one's particular understanding of disembodied intelligence. While transferring HI usually requires transferring the entire person, transactions of AI may be somewhat easier. When a firm wants to transfer some particular data analytics algorithm, it does not have to transfer a physical product. However, merely transferring the algorithm per se is also difficult. Therefore, it will often result in the transfer of an intangible software solution, which involves some additional features beyond the mere intelligence. In a narrow sense, this transaction would refer to embodied intelligence because the algorithm is embodied in a software solution. In a broader sense, this transaction could also be considered relatively close to a transaction of disembodied intelligence because the additional features may be very limited. Accordingly, the largest part of the intangible good that is transferred is actually AI.

Whatever understanding of disembodied intelligence is used, the core challenge remains the same. The markets for intelligence – at least for most types of intelligence – are relatively far away from perfect economic markets. In particular, the inefficiencies of these markets are often quite high. For example, the transaction costs for hiring human experts in order to strengthen a company's HI are usually high. Moreover, the transaction costs for many markets of AI are still relatively high because the solutions often need to be customized to the particular application, and standards are not yet well developed for many applications. Similar to markets for knowledge, the markets for intelligence are characterized by a limited market transparency. While the transaction costs will decrease in many fields of AI over the next years with a growing emergence of standard solutions and standard interfaces, the imperfections of the markets for intelligence will continue, at least in comparison with relatively efficient markets, such as financial markets.

With regard to HI, it is often a challenge to hire the most suitable external experts for intelligence-based reasons. While it may be difficult to measure the different types of HI, especially in the process of selecting new talent, it may be even more challenging to attract the most appropriate persons if multiple types of intelligence are relevant. From an intelligence-based perspective, a person usually is not only hired for one specific type of intelligence, such as creative intelligence. Rather, there will be an interplay of multiple types of intelligence that are needed for performing a given job. On this basis, there will typically be some need for making trade-offs and balancing the different types of HI that are needed for the job and that a candidate offers. Moreover, a new employee may actively shape the job and tasks based on his or her particular set of intelligence. Consequently, firms may deliberately transform and extend their intelligence architecture by hiring talent with specific types of intelligence, but there are substantial imperfections in the markets for HI.

Concerning AI, the markets for transferring intelligence are currently becoming more efficient. While the majority of the transactions is based on AI that is embodied in particular solutions, de facto standards emerge for different fields, and these standards as well as their interfaces enable more efficient transactions of embodied AI. For example, there is an increasing number of planning and optimization solutions which fulfill similar roles and which can be customized to suit a company's particular needs quite easily. The same is true for natural language processing and various applications of machine learning. As the markets for these applications mature, typical solutions and packages lead to a greater ease of transactions and to a higher transparency concerning price levels. Overall, this evolution of the markets leads to a reduction of transaction costs due to market imperfections. This evolution is expected to continue over the next years for a variety of AI applications. The growing markets for embodied AI enable companies to achieve a competitive advantage that is at least partly based on AI, even if the company is not internally developing new AI solutions.

In particular, this type of competitive advantage that is partly based on AI derives from a smart combination of relatively standard AI solutions with other components of a company's intelligence architecture. Moreover, firms may attempt to rely on the markets for HI to strengthen their expertise in AI – with the goal of enhancing the interplay of particular types of HI and AI. Specifically, companies may rely on the markets for HI to hire AI talents. The markets for AI experts are characterized by the same difficulties as the markets for other types of talents. In addition, however, the imperfections of these markets are currently increased by the extreme shortage of AI experts. In light of the advances of various fields of AI, many companies have started AI initiatives, and they have hired – or have tried to hire – new talents for their particular strategic focus in AI. Because of the imperfections in the markets for intelligence, new AI experts are not available immediately. Therefore, there are enormous fights for the top talents. While this is beneficial for the AI experts, it limits many firms' possibilities to strengthen their AI expertise by hiring new employees that would bring the relevant knowhow.

With respect to meta-intelligence, it is even more difficult for a company to rely on the markets for intelligence. The term meta-intelligence refers to the transformation of a firm's intelligence architecture. Consequently, it strongly depends on the particular organization and context. Thus, it is difficult to acquire any particular solutions, consultants or other experts that immediately boost the meta-intelligence. Rather, organizational learning and second-order learning are critical for developing the meta-intelligence, and individual human experts or AI solutions may only provide a minor contribution unless they are integrated with further parts of the intelligence architecture. This is true for large organizations, whereas in a young startup company with five employees, for example, one more person with complementary skills may contribute to the level of HI and indirectly also to the level of the meta-intelligence. Nonetheless, the possibilities for transferring the meta-intelligence are very limited in most situations because it is strongly embedded in the organization and developed along a firm's evolutionary path.

Despite these difficulties in enhancing HI, AI, and especially the meta-intelligence through the markets for intelligence, executives should attempt to benefit from the growth of these markets. With an increasing number of market participants, e. g. human experts for AI, some of the market imperfections will be reduced. Moreover, the growing standardization of AI solutions will ease further transactions, contributing to an additional growth of the markets. Jointly, these trends will lead to a virtuous cycle of growing markets for intelligence with a particular emphasis on AI. These markets offer new strategic opportunities, while the overall opportunities and threats from the advances of AI persist. Consequently, executives should thoroughly analyze the possible benefits from suitable market transactions because they enlarge the strategy space for their companies. Notwithstanding the growth of the markets for intelligence, there will always be significant imperfections in these markets. While these imperfections aggravate market transactions, they simultaneously enhance a company's possibilities to gain and sustain an intelligence-based competitive advantage. In particular, competitors will have a hard time to substitute or imitate a company's intelligence architecture by means of market transactions.

Sustainability of competitive advantage

Gaining an intelligence-based competitive advantage is a major challenge, but sustaining this advantage over time is yet another story. The sustainability of competitive advantage depends on how easily a firm's success drivers can be replicated by competitors.[2] In light of the relatively limited efficiency of the markets for intelligence, competitors may attempt to either substitute or imitate a company's different types of intelligence.[3] Regarding substitution, competitors may, for example, try to arrive at innovative solutions to replace a firm's HI. However, a firm's intelligence architecture typically includes some level of creative destruction, which facilitates the development of new products, services, and business models. Thus, it is often highly challenging to make a firm's intelligence-based efforts and outputs obsolete. These challenges are illustrated by the typical difficulties in inventing around existing patented innovations.[4] Under particular conditions, it may be easier to replace specific AI solutions, but competitors' chances of substituting a firm's different types of intelligence are often relatively limited.

Accordingly, the sustainability of an intelligence-based competitive advantage hinges on competitors' opportunities for imitating rather than substituting for a firm's intelligence-based outputs. Following the strategic management logic of Ingemar Dierickx and Karel Cool, imitability is limited by time compression diseconomies, asset mass efficiencies, intercon nectedness of asset stocks, asset erosion, and causal ambiguity of a company's different types of intelligence, including HI, AI, and meta-intelligence. The presence of time compression diseconomies in intelligence-based activities implies that maintaining a given rate of intelligence effort over a time period produces a larger output than maintaining twice this effort over half the period.[5] Thus, competitors' opportunities to quickly erode a company's intelligence-based competitive advantage may be limited. Moreover, there may well be asset mass efficiencies, which point to increasing returns to scale in intelligence-based activities and to the benefits of combining multiple types of intelligence inside the company, even if a company is strongly involved in external partnerships, networks, and ecosystems.

The interdependencies of the different types of intelligence further aggravate the imitability of intelligence-based competitive advantage drawing on the interconnectedness of asset stocks. For instance, the creative intelligence of a company's R&D experts in developing new products and processes involving AI could be strengthened by insights that have been gained based on the interpersonal intelligence of sales and service employees, who provide essential customer insights for future development activities.[6] Competitors' benefits from imitating a company's intelligence are further reduced because of asset erosion processes. For example, human expertise in particular fields as well as AI solutions may depreciate over time because of technological obsolescence. While these processes erode competitors' benefits from imitation, they also underscore the need for constant renewal and recombination to sustain a competitive advantage. Finally, the causal ambiguity of a complex intelligence architecture aggravates its imitation.[7] Causal ambiguity is further strengthened by the interdependencies of the different types of HI and AI as well as by the context-specificity of the meta-intelligence.

Based on the difficulties of substituting and imitating a firm's intelligence architecture, meta-intelligence provides particular opportunities for sustaining a competitive advantage. On the one hand, the intertemporal nature of renewing and recombining the different types of HI and AI is automatically directed towards sustaining an intelligence-based competitive advantage over time. On the other hand, the complexity and organizational specificity of meta-intelligence further reduces competitors' possibilities for imitation or substitution. In addition, the meta-intelligence is key for designing and adapting a firm's intelligence architecture so that the distinct types of HI and AI contribute to realizing a competitive advantage in alignment with corporate strategy. As such, the meta-intelligence is critical for developing intelligence-based core competencies. However, firms will be unable to excel in all types of intelligence. Rather, they need to focus their intelligence development on those types of HI and AI that appear particularly promising as a basis for achieving a competitive advantage.

In this respect, managers have to consider the following two dimensions: potential core competence and future competitive relevance. On the one hand, it is important to analyze whether an intelligence type may become a core competence. Basically, all types of HI, AI, and the meta-intelligence may have the role of a core competence, but firms will be unable to develop all intelligence types to a competence level that enables a core competence. Reasons for these limitations are, for example, resource constraints and competitors' strategic actions, which usually limit a company's possibilities to outperform competitors in a large variety of intelligences. On the other hand, executives need to examine the future competitive relevance of the specific type of intelligence. In light of the substantial transformation of many industries, the competitive impact of some intelligence types may increase or decrease. Thus, executives need to consider the future strategic relevance of a particular type of intelligence and to adjust the development of this type of intelligence accordingly.

The development of the appropriate competence levels in the different types of intelligence strongly depends on a company's strategy and on the environmental context. Based on the distinction of the two dimensions of potential core competencies and future strategic relevance, executives may think about developing the competence levels in terms of four generic strategies. First, if an intelligence does not have the potential for a core competence and if the future competitive relevance is low, executives may largely neglect this intelligence. Rather than completely ignoring it, however, a well-developed meta-intelligence regularly considers all intelligence types to potentially reevaluate their future importance. Nonetheless, executives should focus on nurturing other types of intelligence if one particular type combines a low competitive relevance and a limited potential for becoming a core competence.

Second, if the future strategic relevance of an intelligence type is high, but the potential for being turned into a core competence is limited, the strategic options are somewhat more complex. Executives should not neglect this intelligence, but they do not need to invest substantial internal resources and executive attention to the internal improvement of this intelligence. Rather, potential partnerships with external parties may be a smart way to build up higher competence levels in this intelligence. If a company's chances of achieving a core competence based on this intelligence are limited anyway, there is no need to exclusively enhance this intelligence internally. Close collaborations with external services providers, other firms in the same industry, or other partners may offer suitable strategic avenues for developing the necessary level of this intelligence for future competition. At the same time, this outside-in approach helps to avoid excessive investments in terms of resources and executive attention in light of limited possibilities for achieving a core competence.

Third, the future strategic relevance of an intelligence type may be limited, but the potential for developing it into a core competence may be relatively high. In this scenario, executives need to explore ways to enhance the strategic importance of this intelligence type in interplay with the firm's strategy. For example, a company may try to transform and redirect the intelligence type in order to enhance the level of related intelligence types, which have a higher competitive relevance. This cross-pollination may work among multiple types of HI and AI. In addition, executives may try to develop markets and competitive conditions under which the particular intelligence plays an important role. These strategic moves assume the availability of a valuable asset, whose value can only be captured if it meets specific conditions. This inside-out perspective suggests creating markets, applications, and use cases where the type of intelligence is fully exploited as a basis for a core competence – which implies a high level of competitive relevance, of course.

Fourth and finally, a particular type of intelligence may have a high strategic relevance in the future and a high potential for becoming a core competence. In this scenario, the type of intelligence should be further developed to achieve a level that actually enables a core competence. On this basis, executives need to address all potential ways of fully leveraging the competitive potential of this intelligence type. This strategic logic includes a thorough analysis of potential means to exclude others from developing similar levels of this intelligence. For example, this may involve specific programs and incentives to enhance the loyalty of key experts in terms of HI or a proprietary use of a valuable algorithm despite higher costs in the case of AI. Full executive attention is well deserved by the intelligence types with these characteristics. These intelligence types provide the basis for gaining a competitive advantage, and their careful development further offers opportunities for sustaining this competitive advantage over relatively long periods.

Sources of competitive advantage

The markets for intelligence and their particular characteristics enable an intelligence-based competitive advantage. In light of the inefficiencies of these markets and the determinants of sustainable competitive positions, firms may in fact achieve distinctly intelligence-based competitive advantages. These advantages may be realized based on the different strategies for developing intelligences to a level that provides a basis for a core competence. So far, the discussion of meta-intelligence suggests that it offers particular opportunities for achieving a sustainable competitive advantage. In general, however, what are the sources for an intelligence-based competitive advantage? As many companies do not yet proficiently manage the interplay of HI and AI, these interfaces provide another important source for an intelligence-based competitive advantage. Specifically, the intelligence-based view of company performance points to five categories of sources of competitive advantage: HI, AI, the integration of HI and AI, the renewal of intelligences, and the recombination of intelligences.[8]

First, many companies continue to strongly invest in the development of specific human expertise. As such, they aim to further strengthen their

HI, which will remain a key factor for achieving an intelligence-based competitive advantage in the future. This focus on superior HI applies to technology-driven companies, but also to companies from many other sectors. For example, the German industry giant Siemens tries to better leverage the unique knowhow of its human experts for the specific requirements of its customers by means of design thinking approaches. At the same time, Siemens relies on the lean startup approach in its startup initiative called Next47 in order to translate particular human expertise in collaboration with external partners into promising business models even faster. While Siemens is also very active in multiple fields of AI, the company continues to strengthen its HI, and it has established multiple initiatives in order to better exploit this particular human expertise.

Second, companies may achieve a competitive advantage primarily by means of a targeted use of AI. While some human factor is also relevant in these AI activities, the competitive focus may be on utilizing AI to outperform competitors. For example, the European insurance company Allianz has implemented a smartphone application called Damage Express. In the case of an insurance claim, customers may use the application to send pictures from their smartphone camera to their vehicle insurance. On this basis, they will receive a response within just one hour, for example a repair order. To be able to offer this service, Allianz strongly relies on AI for image recognition and computer enabled 3D models. Human experts primarily focus on checking the decision that the AI suggests. For Allianz, this application offers efficiency benefits in processing claims. It further provides the customers with an enhanced and expedited service. Consequently, the AI-based innovation substantially exceeds a mere optimization of existing processes.

Third, competitive advantages may emerge at interfaces by combining HI and AI. For example, the company ThinkOwl has more than 20 years of experience in software development related to AI. On this basis, ThinkOwl has developed a service desk software which includes multiple AI technologies and which is able to adapt to the specific workflows of employees. Accordingly, relatively ordinary service inquiries can be answered automatically because the software continuously learns from the work and results of the human employees. At the same efficiency level, the service employees therefore have more time for specific inquiries that need to be processed individually. Here, the software also supports the human experts as much as possible. In many cases, clients of ThinkOwl can implement an enhanced service level and service experience for their customers at lower costs.

Fourth, a competitive advantage may result specifically from the renewal of different types of intelligence. Thus, this category of potential competitive advantages refers to the meta-intelligence. For example, many banks use AI to offer their customers personalized financial planning. In this regard, AI may either extend the personal customer relationship or contribute to the automation of services. AI provides further opportunities for completely new solutions, for example to prevent fraud and money laundering in financial transactions. By continuously renewing the intelligence that is used in critical processes, banks may achieve significant improvements in customer experience and process optimization. Consequently, the transformation of the intelligence architecture towards a stronger use of AI currently constitutes a major driver of innovation in the financial services industry. On this basis, the renewal of the intelligences at the level of the meta-intelligence may provide a major source of superior performance.

Fifth, companies may gain a competitive advantage by reconfiguring their intelligence architecture. This category of potential advantages also refers to the meta-intelligence. However, it describes situations where the different types of HI and AI remain largely unchanged, whereas there are substantial changes in the intelligence architecture. For example, the German telecommunications provider Deutsche Telekom has presented particular guidelines for using AI. In these guidelines, the company clarifies its perspective that AI is targeted at extending human abilities instead of restricting them. Thus, AI may support human actions for achieving a competitive advantage from a close collaboration of AI and human experts. For example, Deutsche Telekom collaborates with the company BS2 to combine AI and further technologies in an early-warning system for the condition of bridges, tunnels, and other buildings. By recombining the available intelligence, the maintenance of important infrastructure is enabled even before any problems are visible from the outside.

Many companies try to use AI to achieve a competitive advantage, even though the focus is often quite exclusively on increasing efficiency. In contrast, the opportunities for developing completely new solutions for the customers are largely neglected. Besides this overemphasis on optimization, many companies do not exploit potential competitive advantages because they focus on the relatively isolated use of AI in addition to the continuous improvement of their HI. However, these approaches only allow for addressing those two sources for competitive advantage that refer to the separate use of HI and AI. The other three sources for competitive advantage, by contrast, are located at the interfaces of HI and AI, and they are largely overlooked by many companies. Therefore, executives need to acknowledge the role of the meta-intelligence in capturing the potential competitive advantages that result from integrating, renewing, and recombining HI and AI. In a future competitive environment, businesses will need Intelligence^x – encompassing multiple types of AI and HI as well as the meta-intelligence. On this basis, executives should analyze the five sources of potential competitive advantage. However, this is only a first step that requires an effective implementation of the selected strategies.

 Chapter 9

Value creation and value capture

Many companies have difficulties in designing suitable strategic responses to the recent advances in AI and related technology fields. In fact, many businesses have been relatively slow in starting their digital transformation in the past years. As a consequence, they are still involved in leveraging the new digital opportunities and the data that they now collect. Some companies are not yet ready for the next level by implementing AI solutions – although this AI implementation could be a major step towards profiting from the data that is collected as a result of the digital transformation initiatives. Nonetheless, a relatively strong reluctance to implement AI may currently be observed in companies from various sectors. This is true for all types of AI solutions, including tools for enhancing the efficiency of internal processes. In particular, however, this reluctance may be observed for AI solutions that would involve a substantial transformation of a firm's internal activities and processes to develop and to commercialize new products and services.

What is the reason for the limited attention given to AI in many companies, especially concerning the insufficient combination of digital and non-digital innovation to arrive at novel solutions? A central driver of businesses' imbalanced approaches to AI is the underlying managerial logic. The executives in most companies develop strategies in response to AI based on their established managerial logics.[1] These dominant logics highlight the role of executives' cognitive structures and processes, which influence business definitions as well as companies' strategic initiatives, such as AI and digitalization. In this regard, a dominant logic is a cognitive frame for strategizing that provides an information filter that influences strategy development and implementation. A relatively strong filter, which implies a narrow bandwidth of the dominant managerial logic, is often developed at the level of individual executives who accumulate experience in a relatively narrow competitive environment, which leads to the reinforcement of established business procedures, success factors, and investment decisions, which proved to be suitable in the past.

Beyond individual executives, however, a dominant managerial logic often becomes particularly pronounced in groups and organizational units. A company's top management team may develop a strong managerial logic because the experiences of multiple members reinforce one another. As such, the dominant logic leads to additional decisions and actions that further strengthen this established wisdom. Over time, this leads to a self-reinforcing spiral of actions influencing executive thinking and vice versa. Opinions of outsiders beyond the core group will be considered in less detail even if such experts – from within or outside the firm – provide important new data, information, knowledge, and intelligence. However, the strong information filter of the dominant logic leads to limited attention to completely new perspectives. If this filter is too narrow, a company is likely to miss important opportunities which may finally result in rigidity and inertia, especially with respect to completely new solutions and business models.[2]

While this potential for inertia exists in all transformation and change processes, it is particularly pronounced in disruptive transformation processes, which may often result from AI implementation. This limited awareness and openness to new business models is a central barrier to successfully coping with the managerial challenges of AI because the most disruptive effect often is the transformation of business models, which goes beyond the mere adaptation of internal processes. In fact, executives need to understand that the disruptive nature of AI primarily derives from new business models, for example based on data analytics or integrated solution providers, which downgrade established manufacturers to mere hardware suppliers. Most of these completely novel solutions require a combination of AI and non-digital innovations, especially business model innovations. This is a central challenge in many fields of digitalization, such as autonomous driving, smart home, digital health, and logistics. For example, many airlines, such as Germany's Lufthansa Group, pursue big data and further analytics approaches to better understand their customers and to offer them customized solutions, which may involve completely new products and services.[3]

In contrast, many executives tend to focus on the established strategies and procedures in their companies in light of disruptive evolutionary changes. This move towards considering well-known competitive environments is typical for a dominant managerial logic. Many executives have spent most of their professional careers in relatively homogeneous environments. Of course, these environments have undergone some major changes, but the underlying business logic in terms of success factors for achieving a competitive advantage has remained largely similar over considerable periods of time. These environments have often been dynamic, but the need for disruptive strategic moves was often relatively low. Consequently, the executives have accumulated substantial expertise in these competitive environments. This significant expertise may partly help them, but it may also constitute a major barrier to acknowledging the need for change and to implementing strategic responses subsequently.

Above all, a dominant managerial logic influences the way in which executives conceptualize a company's business, which in turn dramatically affects the very beginning of strategic planning processes concerning new opportunities and threats. As such, the dominant logic will influence executives' perception of AI at different conceptual levels, including data, information, knowledge, and intelligence. For example, data about the advances in AI is interpreted in light of the dominant managerial logic. In a similar vein, information about implementation challenges for specific AI solutions is processed by the dominant logic's information filter. Moreover, the knowledge base of the executives will affect their strategic decisions about the scope and timing of AI initiatives in their companies. Furthermore, the available HI and AI are influenced by the dominant managerial logic, which will affect analyses and strategic responses about implementing AI solutions and about integrating AI and HI. Consequently, the dominant managerial logic is a powerful roadblock or enabler of AI implementation.

Overemphasis on technology

The dominant managerial logic may limit a company's adoption of AI solutions. Even if it does not affect the scope of utilizing AI, it may influence the type of solutions that are selected and the way how AI is implemented and potentially integrated with HI. In particular, a strong managerial logic may lead to interpreting the recent advances in AI in terms of established business procedures and success factors. As a consequence, AI is often viewed as a new technological opportunity that may be exploited in the context of a company's established business. This assessment of AI is generally not wrong, but it is also only part of a more complex story – and part of a more substantial strategic impact, which may in fact have a disruptive nature in many industries. However, this transformation of the industry and underlying business logic is often insufficiently considered in companies that are characterized by a strong managerial logic of the top management team. In addition, the potential for combining HI and AI is usually not examined in detail in these companies. Accordingly, the opportunities of integrated intelligence remain largely unrealized.

Rather, executives in these companies often directly address the technology issues that are associated with a relatively isolated implementation of particular AI solutions. In fact, the dominant logic in these companies often leads to AI being considered a new software tool. In contrast, the market-based opportunities and threats are not assessed in depth. In addition, executives in companies with a strong managerial logic are often not willing to substantially change the intelligence architecture of their organization. Accordingly, new AI solutions are used, but their implementation focuses on replacing some components of HI or simply adding the AI solutions to the established intelligence architecture. Thus, there may be a limited level of intelligence renewal, whereas there is hardly any recombination of the different types of intelligence. A substantial recombination would often question the underlying managerial logic, and it would require a transformation of a company's logic and business model. Accordingly, there is only a limited tendency to undergo these substantial changes.

Based on a view of AI primarily in terms of the dominant managerial logic and established intelligence architecture, many companies start their

AI initiatives by analyzing the technological challenges. After developing a basic understanding of the relevance of AI for their established business, many companies immediately start selecting a particular supplier of AI solutions. Accordingly, these companies directly focus on the IT challenges. After selecting a solution provider, a specific AI solution is developed or customized to the requirements of the company. Typically, the solution is adapted to some degree to a company's situation. However, it usually does not consider the company's entire established intelligence architecture. As such, it often is impossible to leverage the interdependencies between the AI solution and a company's other types of intelligence. Then, the solution is implemented, and it is used in a company's internal processes. Usually, the focus is on enhancing the efficiency of established procedures.

Of course, a stronger use of AI also involves major technological challenges, and the recent advances in AI can largely be traced back to the overall technological evolution. An overemphasis on these technological challenges, especially software solutions, may be a natural move in light of a dominant managerial logic – but it may often lead to ineffective AI implementation. As such, it may even have negative competitive effects because it leads to reinforcing a company's established business model and business processes, which are only polished by implementing a few selected AI solutions. Consequently, a significant transformation of the intelligence architecture is blocked because at first glance the company may even appear to be among the leading companies in terms of AI implementation. Instead of helping the firm to advance to the next level of the evolution of its intelligence architecture, the quick implementation of specific AI solutions may rather reinforce the status quo.

Paradoxically, the positive strategic intent of implementing AI solutions may actually backfire if a strong managerial logic only enables a relatively superficial implementation of some selected AI solutions. Thus, directly jumping to the selection of an IT provider often is not a suitable way to tackle AI. In contrast to pursuing a balanced strategic approach, an immediate focus on IT challenges may limit the impact of AI initiatives to enhancing efficiency. The growth opportunities of bundling digital and non-digital innovation are neglected. Consequently, any AI initiative needs to involve business model and strategy experts from the very beginning instead of exclusively relying on IT experts. Rather than having business models emerge by the time of implementing AI solutions, business model design has to occur at the very beginning of an AI initiative, and it has to consider non-digital innovations, such as new products and services. On this basis, companies will be able to fully profit from the optimization and growth opportunities of AI rather than merely defending the established business by strengthening efficiency with new IT solutions.

Major technological advances drive the recent evolution towards AI, but the core managerial challenges for businesses often do not reside in the technology domain. An excessive emphasis on technological issues may therefore be detrimental, especially in the beginning of AI initiatives. With good intentions, executives may quickly move ahead towards AI implementation, often underscoring the importance of speeding up execution by means of an agile approach. While agility is in fact beneficial in the implementation of AI initiatives, it is equally important to allow for sufficient time and resources to enable a comprehensive strategic analysis of the growing possibilities of AI, including the potential transformation of a company's intelligence architecture and recombination of multiple types of intelligence. This does not mean that executives should not speed up the implementation of selected AI applications, following an agile approach. However, merely focusing on a few IT solutions does not consider the real competitive impact of AI, which goes far beyond these technological consequences. Therefore, executives at least need to balance a broad and detailed strategic assessment of AI opportunities and threats with an agile implementation of selected AI solutions in order to achieve some quick wins in terms of profiting from AI.

Importance of the business model

The business model is key for understanding the competitive impact of AI on companies in many different sectors. While many executives focus on the technological changes, the market-related changes are at least equally important. The management challenges that result from these technology push and market pull effects culminate in their effects on the business model. The business model goes beyond a firm's strategy and helps to consider changes in the overall industry value chain as well as changes of the relevant stakeholders in the ecosystem. Accordingly, it helps to understand and to map the impact of AI on a company's business activities. Changing the business model often involves transforming the dominant managerial logic. This is a major difference between business model innovations and other types of innovation, such as new products, processes, or services. While product, service, and process innovations often occur within a company's dominant managerial logic, a substantial business model innovation may well question the established managerial logic.

In light of a relatively strong dominant logic in their organizations, many executives neglect a systematic assessment of the full business model implications of AI. Basically, a business model comprises three core parts.[4] First, a company's business model includes the value proposition. Thus, it describes what gain points and paint points of a company's customers are addressed. Second, the business model describes a company's value creation activities. These activities comprise internal organizational procedures and external relationships in the business ecosystem. Third, the business model addresses the value capture activities. In particular, this part describes the revenue model. As such, it helps to understand how a company may actually appropriate some of the value that is created based on the value proposition and value creation activities. By integrating value proposition, value creation, and value capture, the business model is critical for understanding and designing AI initiatives because AI may affect all three components of established business models.

Many effects of AI on a company's business model are positive. For example, AI may enable new value propositions for a firm's customers. In addition, it may provide the basis for enhanced value creation by strengthening the effectiveness and efficiency of a company's business processes. Furthermore, AI may allow for capturing additional value, for example by optimizing a company's revenue streams and cash flows. As such, there are multiple opportunities for strengthening a company's business model by implementing different AI solutions. At the same time, however, AI may also pose various threats to established business models. Many of these threats depend on the particular type of AI. For instance, machine learning or robotics may substantially transform a company's business model by replacing some part of human activity. While this reduces human value creation in some parts of the company, it also enables new entrants to attack a company's competitive position in its traditional markets. These potential new entrants often do not have a legacy organization and IT infrastructure, and they may set up leaner processes than the existing companies. Accordingly, a company's established business model may be immediately at risk.

While these threats to a firm's business model are relatively specific to the particular type of AI, there is another overarching tendency that may be observed in many industries based on a combination of multiple types of AI as well as additional digital technologies. This central threat for many established companies is the cannibalization of their customer access by digital solution providers, who rely on AI and related technologies in order to provide an integrated digital solution to a firm's customers. As such, these solution providers may occupy the interface between an established company and its customers – with potentially detrimental effects on the business model and financial performance of the company. Accordingly, AI may lead to situations where established businesses that develop and commercialize physical products are downgraded to mere providers of hardware, whereas the downstream link to their customers – and all the value that is created at this interface – is taken over by digital service providers.[5]

In fact, AI plays a central role in the business models of many platform providers, such as Amazon, Google, and booking.com. The digital platforms strongly rely on AI in order to continuously enhance their customer experience as well as customer knowledge. On this basis, they cannibalize the customer access and customer data of established hardware manufacturers. In the context of decreasing revenues in the business that is not based on the digital platforms, most of these companies need to collaborate with the platform providers, but this collaboration will further intensify the dependency on this partner – or competitor. Depending on the particular use case, a company may actually face multiple potential solution providers. In the future, the company will still have a running business, but the margins will usually deteriorate if solution providers capture a significant portion of the value that is offered to the customers at the very end of the value chain. Over time, the solution providers can further optimize their own business models by using AI for analyzing the detailed customer data that they collect. Consequently, the offers of the solution providers will further improve, leading to the situation that the solution providers capture an additional portion of the overall value.

Digital platforms only represent the tip of the iceberg of new business models based on AI and other digital technologies. Most of these platforms do not offer any own hardware products, but they merely focus on connecting established products and assets in a meaningful way for customers based on leveraging AI and further software solutions. Beyond digital platforms, similar effects may be observed across multiple sectors. In all of these industries, new or established players emerge to integrate multiple products and components with intangible services and AI to offer customers optimal solutions for their particular use cases. These developments may currently be observed in many manufacturing industries, including machinery, chemicals, electronics, logistics, and retail. The complexity of digital solutions that include – but are not based exclusively on – AI enable new business models as an integration provider. If a company is not in the position to become a solution provider, it is at least essential to sketch a sustainable business model, which will enable an advantageous competitive position in the long run despite the emergence of these digital solution providers.

Balancing the business model

To achieve a sustainable competitive advantage in light of a growing importance of AI, executives need to be open to reconsidering their company's business model. One aspect of this is to thoroughly examine the threats from integrated solution providers, which may cannibalize their competitive position in established markets by occupying the customer interface. At the same time, they need to pursue the opportunities that usually emerge from integrating advanced AI solutions in a company's intelligence architecture. Besides balancing opportunities and threats, a thorough assessment of the business model implications also allows for balancing the assessment of technological challenges and market trends rather than excessively concentrating on the technology domain. On this basis, a key task for executives in light of a growing competitive impact of AI is aligning the effects on the value proposition, value creation, and value capture components of the business model – or of multiple new and emergent business models.

At the heart of the business model is the value proposition for a firm's customers. Consistent with the dominant managerial logic, many companies are reluctant to substantially alter or to extend this value proposition. Many executives are open to addressing some additional pain points and gain points of their customers to improve the customer experience. However, this approach typically does not consider the option to completely

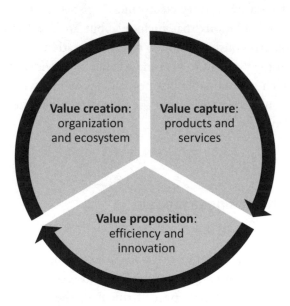

Figure 6: Balancing the business model components

transform the value proposition and business model. This reluctance is a reason why many companies have difficulties finding a profitable competitive position in light of integrated solution providers. Transforming one's own business model towards becoming a solution provider or occupying an attractive spot in the reconfigured industry value chain would often involve a novel value proposition for a company's customers. As the focus of most firms' AI initiatives so far has been on strengthening efficiency, innovation and growth opportunities have mostly been neglected. It is therefore time to complement this efficiency focus and to challenge a company's value proposition in order to achieve innovation and new growth opportunities in light of the growing importance of AI (Figure 6). By providing a value proposition that combines AI and a company's established human expertise, companies may often achieve a sustainable competitive advantage even in light of new entrants that are likely to become integrated solution providers in their established industry.

Beyond the value proposition, AI may strongly affect a company's value creation processes. Here, most companies that implement AI experience considerable changes because the value creation activities are directly affected if AI is used to replace human work in their internal processes. While the optimization of internal processes is a typical focus of AI initiatives, the impact of AI often goes far beyond internal processes. For example, it may also change a company's internal organization and culture, including new leadership principles and HR strategies. Even more important than these internal organizational effects, however, are often the implications for the external business ecosystem. In particular, a successful implementation of AI will typically require collaboration with multiple external partners, such as IT service providers, suppliers of complementary products, integrated logistics providers, and so on. In many cases, these partners have not previously been part of a firm's established business ecosystem. Consequently, many managerial challenges emerge at the interfaces, and executives need to put particular emphasis on balancing the internal organization and the external ecosystem to ensure a smooth value creation across multiple internal and external stages.

In terms of the value capture part of the business model, AI may also lead to major changes. In particular, advanced data analytics often ena ble new solutions, which go considerably beyond a company's established hardware products. In many cases, these solutions exceed the established service portfolio. The bundling of products and services with novel insights from data analytics leads to new and intelligent solutions for a company's customers. Consequently, a company's revenue model may often undergo notable changes because of AI. In the past, many companies already experienced substantial difficulties in transforming their product-driven business towards a more service-centered approach. A further bundling of multiple tangible and intangible components towards solutions constitutes yet another level, and it often requires transformation processes in multiple steps to simultaneously match the needs of internal and external stakeholders. AI is often embodied in products and services, but the real value for a customer comes from the integrated intelligence. Consequently, the value capture part of the business model needs to design the revenue streams based on the underlying value that is provided by intelligence rather than by products and services per se.

In sum, AI often involves major alterations to the value creation and value capture parts of business models. In addition, it often enables completely new value propositions. Thus, AI may affect all three parts of the business model – at the level of an individual company, but also at the level of overall value creation and value capture activities in an entire sector. Thus, executives need to acknowledge the potentially limiting nature of their own managerial logics. This is particularly important if these logics are strongly shared among the top management team. By examining the entire business model, executives can avoid the typical mistake of focusing immediately on the technological challenges of implementing AI. At the same time, the business model perspective facilitates moving beyond AI and considering the overall intelligence architecture in an integrated way. The more integrated new AI solutions are with the remaining parts of a company's intelligence architecture, the more sustainable the business model typically is. To achieve a sustainable competitive advantage from AI, executives therefore need to align the internal organization and external ecosystems.

Part D

Organization

Chapter 10

Internal organization and external ecosystems

A company's different types of intelligence are strongly based on internal organizational characteristics. However, businesses cannot accumulate all relevant intelligence internally, and this is true even for the largest multinational companies. Therefore, external factors, such as the competitive ecosystem, also play a role for understanding and developing a company's intelligence architecture. The distinction between internal and external factors that drive a company's intelligence appears quite ordinary from a strategy development and strategy execution point of view. Nonetheless, designing a company's organization and its boundaries often constitutes a complex challenge from an intelligence-based perspective. In this regard, an intelligence-based view assumes that company boundaries are designed to maximize the benefits from the different types of intelligence.[1] Companies decide whether an activity is best accomplished within their organizational boundaries or through the markets for intelligence based on the benefits and costs of these options with regard to company performance.[2]

In recent years, a trend towards outsourcing various activities, such as production, could be observed in many companies. Despite this overall outsourcing trend, there is a need for developing a company's internal intelligence architecture because a complete outsourcing of intelligence is hardly possible and most likely detrimental. The intelligence architecture is at the very core of companies, and its complexity requires the coordinated efforts of multiple specialists. The markets for intelligence are often unable to perform this coordinating function for at least the following three reasons. First, a company's different types of intelligence often include some degree of novelty, especially when they are combined to form a company's entire intelligence architecture. As such, the variety of intelligence types often cannot be acquired through the market. Second, the marketing of many intelligence types entails the risk of disclosing their relevant characteristics to others.[3] These difficulties can partly be reduced by intellectual property rights, but many appropriability challenges remain. Third, the specificity and complexity of many intelligence types typically leads to the need for major adaptations if they are acquired from the market. For instance, the creative intelligence of employees or specific machine learning algorithms need to be thoroughly tailored to a firm's specific requirements to ensure sufficient fit with the organization.

For these and other reasons, the markets for intelligence are often inefficient, and companies need to find suitable ways to profit from external intelligence. Thus, companies fulfill an important function by integrating the different types of intelligence of multiple members, and they need to achieve fit between their intelligence architecture and organizational characteristics. As such, the different types of intelligence provide the opportunity for sustaining superior performance because they can often not be accessed through the market. The market inefficiencies are particularly severe for meta-intelligence, which involves the renewal and recombination of the different intelligence types. Because of this transformational nature, the meta-intelligence is usually closely tied to a company's particular situation, and it can hardly be transferred effectively to other organizations. Thus, the need for internally building up the meta-intelligence is assumed to be even higher than for the other types of intelligence, which can draw more on external drivers in a company's environment.

Boundaries of the company

To specify organizational boundaries, it is helpful to address four related issues concerning the virtues and failures of companies and markets.[4] First, an intelligence-based view assumes that markets work relatively well for many standard activities and products with a limited level of intelligence. Second, markets fail as a form of governance for many components, products, and services with higher levels of intelligence for the reasons outlined above. As a consequence, the markets for intelligence are inefficient relative to many other markets, such as financial markets. Third, an intelligence-based perspective suggests that internal governance in an organization works relatively well for many types of intelligence because a complete outsourcing of the intelligence architecture is usually impossible. Fourth, many organizations fail to conduct all activities that are critical for developing their intelligence architecture internally because of the variety of expertise that is needed for the different types of intelligence. Thus, many companies rely on relationships with other organizations for strengthening their intelligence architecture.

As such, an intelligence-based view explicitly considers the trend towards external networks, open innovation, and co-creation. To increasingly collaborate with external partners and to draw on external intelligence, companies rely on a variety of mechanisms, such as crowdsourcing, R&D alliances, user integration, and various types of intelligence intermediaries. However, a strong involvement in external networks is not a new trend, nor does it challenge arguments emphasizing the relative inefficiency of markets for intelligence. Hybrid forms of coordinating the intelligence architecture, such as strategic alliances, continue to increase, but they usually constitute complements to rather than substitutes for the internal intelligence architecture. Despite this trend towards opening up a firm's intelligence architecture, critical types of intelligence continue to be coordinated inside a company's boundaries. This perspective is consistent with resource-based arguments because even firms that strongly rely on collaborations with other companies conduct the essential activities of orchestrating their networks internally.

Moreover, the idiosyncratic nature of a firm's position in an extended intelligence network may provide the basis for sustainable superior performance because the efficiency of general markets for intelligence will remain limited relative to many other markets. The increasingly collaborative character of many companies' intelligence architectures does not reduce the key role of internal intelligence because the collaborations with external partners complement the internal architecture. As AI offers new opportunities for extending a company's intelligence architecture beyond its organizational boundaries, it may actually strengthen the relevance of the different types of intelligence for company performance. It further calls for revising a firm's internal activities towards orchestrating external ecosystems, and many companies may evolve from integrated intelligence generators towards interconnected intelligence brokers because they strongly build on internal and external sources for their different types of intelligence.

Thus, an intelligence-based view complements many existing boundary conceptions by explicitly considering that intelligence spans organizational borders. A company is embedded in an ecosystem, which includes, for example, complementary types of intelligence at other organizations. As such, the ecosystem is often not aligned with traditional industry boundaries, and this view helps to overcome a rigid understanding of an endogenous internal organization and an exogenous external environment. Firms usually face internal restrictions on designing their intelligence architecture because of path dependencies in the development of the intelligence types. At the same time, an intelligence-based view underscores companies' ability to actively shape their environment to achieve fit with their intelligence types – even if attempts to shape the environment are very challenging and complex. For instance, organizations may not only attempt to influence their ecosystem, but they may also try to shape the appropriability regime and the industry structure, which are not completely exogenous.[5] In boundary decisions, organizations generally attempt to maximize the value for their intelligence architecture rather than merely minimizing costs, e. g. transaction costs.[6]

A company's intelligence architecture and the different types of intelligence depend on multiple internal and external factors at various levels. The distinction between internal and external factors helps to systematize the key factors at multiple levels, but it does not mean that the internal factors are endogenous and the external factors are exogenous. Instead, firms may actively influence a subset of the internal and external factors, while the remaining internal and external factors can hardly be influenced for intelligence-related reasons. As it is hardly possible to compile a comprehensive list of all factors that affect a firm's different types of intelligence, the following discussion and Figure 7 provide an illustrative overview.

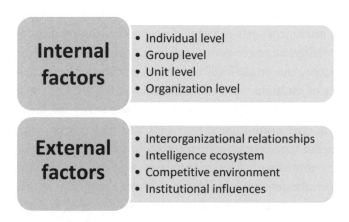

Figure 7: Internal and external factors at multiple levels
(Source: partly adapted from Lichtenthaler, 2016, Management Decision[7])

Internal factors at multiple levels

Regarding the internal factors that drive a company's intelligence architecture, some key factors are located at the individual, group, unit, and organization level. The individual-level factors refer to specific sources of AI and HI that contribute to particular types of intelligence even if they are used in relative isolation rather than being complemented by other factors. With regard to HI, for example, the individual creativity of selected employees may provide a key basis for achieving a competitive advantage. Examples here are R&D departments or marketing agencies. Concerning AI, for example, a particular algorithm may strongly enhance the efficiency of a company's internal processes, and it may be difficult to imitate for competitors. While these factors play a key role at the individual level, they also affect factors at other levels. For example, top human experts in particular fields of AI may enable the selection of the best AI solutions based on the available budget. In turn, these AI solutions may then provide additional advantages. Other examples of individual-level factors are skills of the Chief Executive Officer and intelligence characteristics of other employees. Thus, these individual-level determinants focus on the particular intelligence per se rather than on the combination of multiple types of intelligence or on multiple players with similar intelligences.

In contrast, the group-level factors specifically address these interdependencies of multiple types of intelligence at the level of the team, project, or other groups. As such, the group level is key for leveraging the positive synergies of multiple types of HI and AI. For example, an investment manager may take investment decisions based on prior knowledge, which is combined with AI-based analyses. Accordingly, the specific value derives from the interplay of HI and AI, and there may be situations of pooled, sequential, or reciprocal interdependence. Specifically, there may be interactions among multiple types of HI, interactions among multiple types of AI, and interactions among different types of AI and HI. As such, the group-level factors do not address a single employee's expertise for selecting the most suitable AI solution, which is subsequently implemented in a relatively independent way. Instead, this set of factors refers to combining multiple types of intelligence in specific projects, workflows, communities of practice, and further groups. For example, the complementary intelligence of the top management and the quality of teamwork in innovation projects play an important role here. In addition, the particular attitudes of an organization's employees towards AI may facilitate or hinder the effective implementation of AI solutions.

Intelligence determinants at the unit level are particularly important in large organizations with multiple business units or functional units. In smaller companies, the unit level overlaps with the organizational level. At the unit level, companies also aim at combining different types of AI and HI. In contrast to the group level, however, the focus is not on one specific type of interaction. Instead, companies attempt to integrate multiple types of intelligence in order to achieve particular strategic goals. For example, companies may rely on cognitive analytics and advanced platforms for enterprise search in order to leverage and integrate all the data, information, knowledge, and intelligence that they have at system level in a particular business unit. These tools for integrating different types of intelligence may be considered as evolutions of the traditional market research tools and knowledge management systems of business units. Accordingly, the focus here is on enabling and encouraging the group interactions by providing the necessary infrastructure and context at the level of business units or functional units.

Finally, the organization-level factors refer to those determinants of intelligence that are distinctly organizational. As such, these factors exceed the benefits of integrating multiple types of intelligence at the level of a single business unit or functional unit. For example, companies may profit from synergies by combining the different types of AI and HI in one business unit with some selected AI and HI of another business unit. As such, the overall intelligence architecture in a large company may provide the basis for achieving intelligence-based synergies in multibusiness firms. Similar benefits may be achieved by combining the intelligence from different functional departments. For instance, the market-related intelligence of the marketing department may be integrated with the creative intelligence in the R&D department and advanced analytics from the customer relationship management solution of the sales department in order to optimize the next generation of new products. Moreover, the organizational level is key for developing the meta-intelligence, which helps to renew and recombine the corporate intelligence architecture beyond the different organizational units. In addition, the organization-level factors include organizational culture and company size because larger companies may have some intelligence-based advantages due to a large internal intelligence architecture.

Many of these internal factors can be deliberately influenced to optimize a company's intelligence architecture, whereas some other factors, such as firm size and top management team diversity, can hardly be influenced in the short term in order to strengthen a company's intelligence. Furthermore, there are important bottom-up and top-down processes that shape these internal factors across multiple levels. For example, social integration mechanisms are an important internal factor because they facilitate mutual understanding, which is essential for several of the intelligence determinants. In addition, there may be some similarities, but also important differences between the determinants of various types of intelligence. Selected determinants may positively influence multiple intelligence types, whereas others may positively affect only one type with negative effects on other types. For example, an AI-based tool for idea management may contribute to a firm's creative intelligence, but it may also result in inertia regarding the meta-intelligence by limiting employees' willingness to transform the entire intelligence architecture. Thus, companies need to establish appropriate conditions for each type of intelligence, and they need to establish an intelligence architecture management at the organizational level.

An optimization of the overall intelligence architecture in terms of the entirety of intelligence types is critical because of limited investments in enhancing the intelligence architecture and the interdependencies among the intelligence determinants in many organization. Here, an intelligence-based perspective highlights the interdependencies among the distinct types of intelligence and the meta-intelligence. Depending on the specific strategy, a company will emphasize and deemphasize particular types of intelligence, and it will try to achieve some balance between AI, HI, and meta-intelligence. Based on this particular emphasis, companies attempt to achieve alignment between their intelligence architecture and strategy in the context of multiple context factors. Accordingly, the factors of the different intelligence types are interrelated with a company's strategy. Thus, decisions on the different types of intelligence need to be aligned with a company's strategic emphasis. Over time, an emphasis on particular types of intelligence in alignment with a company's strategy will lead to a specific intelligence architecture, which provides fit with multiple context factors.

External factors at multiple levels

Beyond the internal determinants of the intelligence architecture, a firm's level of the different types of intelligence is also affected by factors beyond organizational boundaries. Of course, the internal factors are key in determining a firm's intelligence architecture. However, even the largest companies will be unable to know everything that they need to know for fully developing their intelligence architecture internally. Consequently, companies may rely on several external factors that determine their level of the different intelligence types. While not all of the external factors may be actively influenced by the firm, executives can undertake many steps to shape the environment in their favor. Consistent with the internal factors, the external factors may be systematized according to different levels of analysis. The list of external factors that are displayed in Figure 7 does not provide a comprehensive description of all relevant factors, but rather offers an illustrative overview. Concerning the external factors that drive a firm's intelligence architecture, some important factors are located at the level of a company's interorganizational relationships, intelligence ecosystem, competitive environment, and institutional influences.

The factors at the level of a firm's interorganizational relationships refer to all types of collaboration that a company currently maintains with external partners. Among those partnerships may be joint ventures, strategic alliances, licensing deals, and many other forms of formal and informal partnerships. From an intelligence-based perspective, companies may use these relationships for accessing external sources of intelligence. Especially, firms may have privileged access to this external intelligence that potential competitors do not have. As such, the external relationships form a company's extended intelligence architecture, which goes beyond its organizational boundaries. For example, companies may leverage the HI of an alliance partner's employees. In addition, the use of AI may involve close relationships with specialized service providers who help a business to fully capture the value of the AI solutions. External partnerships may also provide a key factor for developing the meta-intelligence because a company's network of external ties offers major benefits in terms of flexibility and adaptability to environmental changes. As such, the external relationships ease the renewal and recombination of the multiple types of intelligence.

Beyond the contractual partnerships with other organizations, there are important determinants of a company's intelligence at the level of the intelligence ecosystem. The intelligence ecosystem refers to all stakeholders and parties in a company's environment that play a role from an intelligence-based view. For example, these may be customers, suppliers, and other 'usual suspects', who represent the traditional part of a company's environment. In light of a growing use of AI, however, there are also further stakeholders, who may play a key role. For instance, the providers of complementary services may be important because only their services enable a comprehensive and personalized experience for a company's customers based on advanced analytics of customer data. The importance of complementary solutions is well accepted in the electronics industry, for example with countless apps using the same hardware and underlying operating system. However, it is also relevant in many other industries, including manufacturing where smart production solutions typically include software, components, and services from multiple players, who form a strong ecosystem. On this basis, customers at the end of the value chain often take strategic decisions between different ecosystems rather than between different products or services of a single company.

Factors related to the competitive environment primarily comprise the intelligence-related activities of current competitors and the potential for new competitors entering the market. With regard to current competitors, many companies have a tendency towards imitating some of their strategic decisions and initiatives with regard to AI. In fact, competitors' announcements of moving towards a stronger use of AI have motivated many firms to go into a similar direction even if they were relatively reluctant to start such initiatives in the beginning. However, the fear of competitive drawbacks from a late start in the field of AI often constitutes a relatively strong incentive for investing at least in selected AI applications. From an intelligence-based perspective, it is also important to think beyond a company's current competitors and to consider potential new entrants. These may be companies from other industries, which leverage their existing intelligence into new fields. In addition, startup firms may exploit AI for entering the market by providing a unique value to a company's traditional customers. Here, the threat of integrated solution providers who occupy a firm's customer interface must not be underestimated.

Finally, the institutional influences involve external scientific developments and appropriability conditions, among other factors. The recent advances in basic research and applied development in many fields of AI illustrate the importance of institutional influences. Without these general scientific advances, most current AI initiatives would not be possible. Even if a large part of the improvements of AI applications is undertaken by companies – a larger portion than in many other scientific fields – all companies benefit from the overall growth of the knowledge and intelligence about the different fields of AI. Often, there are strong linkages between the scientific developments of various public and private institutions in a specific field of AI, including universities, research institutes, large multinational companies, and small startups. Nonetheless, most players focus on some particular proprietary insights and intelligence. Here, the appropriability conditions are key. By means of patents and various other protection mechanisms, companies attempt to capture a large part of the value of their internal intelligence and scientific developments. Overall, these environmental factors extend a company's industry and ecosystem, but they may directly affect the development of a company's intelligence.

Some of these external factors can be influenced at least to some degree in order to strengthen a company's intelligence architecture. For example, executives may actively address the emergence of complementary services in the ecosystem and to some degree also the appropriability regime. Here, businesses may try to influence an emerging dominant design with specific interfaces for particular AI solutions. As such, companies may enhance the opportunities for commercializing their own AI solutions. These effects illustrate the possibilities to influence the appropriability of the results of a company's intelligence. Many other factors, such as scientific advances, are largely exogenous with respect to a company's intelligence architecture. In addition, market conditions can only be influenced to a limited degree. However, highly competitive markets may strengthen the effects of multiple external factors on a company's intelligence architecture. Thus, it is useful to consider the external determinants of a company's intelligence architecture. As such, executives may shape the environmental conditions in order to strengthen their company's level of the key intelligence types. This emphasis on selected types of intelligence needs to be aligned with a company's strategy in order to channel the attention to those external factors that are most relevant for the intelligence strategy.

Among the variety of external factors, the interorganizational relationships are key. These partnerships can be actively influenced, and the preferred access to the knowledge and intelligence that are integrated in these networks extends a company's internal intelligence architecture. In light of the inefficiencies in the markets for intelligence, these external partnerships are a major way of accessing the markets. Thus, a company's entire portfolio of alliances and further collaborations needs to be orchestrated to optimize their effects on the intelligence architecture. For example, a company may enter multiple collaborations in order to achieve complementary effects on its internal intelligence. Here, it is helpful to orchestrate the network of relationships to align a company's network position with its strategy for extending the internal intelligence architecture with the external relationships. In particular, a company may try to balance some internal intelligence weaknesses by building up strong external relationships in these fields and vice versa.

Thus, establishing and orchestrating the partnerships and other external factors is important for actively developing a company's intelligence architecture. However, external networks per se are only necessary, but not sufficient for actually enhancing a company's intelligence architecture on this basis. To fully profit from the markets for intelligence, companies need absorptive capacity, which refers to the ability to identify suitable external sources, to acquire the relevant knowledge and intelligence, and to finally utilize this intelligence.[8] Besides this ability for inward knowledge transfer, companies also need to develop desorptive capacity, which refers to a company's ability to spot external opportunities for applying a company's intelligence and to transfer the relevant knowledge to external partners.[9] As many intelligence-based partnerships involve a mutual transfer of HI and AI among the partners, absorptive capacity and desorptive capacity may be critical in order to profit from the external determinants of a company's intelligence architecture.

Otherwise, a company would be involved in external partnerships and ecosystems with limited positive effects on its level of the different types of intelligence. Thus, companies need some prior level of the particular type of intelligence in order to capture the value of external relationships for this intelligence type. These linkages between the internal and external factors underscore the need for an integrative management and design of a company's intelligence architecture. A completely internal development of all types of intelligence will often hardly be possible, and a complete outsourcing of particular types of intelligence is also not an option. Rather, executives need to balance the internal and external factors in order to jointly arrive at a those levels of intelligence that are needed for successfully developing and implementing a company's strategy. In light of the dynamic nature of a company's intelligence architecture, this balancing process is a core part of the meta-intelligence, and it may constitute a major source of intelligence-based competitive advantage.

Chapter 11

The No-Human-Interaction paradox

The full impact of the digital transformation process has not yet materialized in many companies. Consequently, many employees are still getting used to a growing importance of data and software for their established business lines in various industries, such as automotive, chemicals, electronics, machinery, and fast-moving consumer goods. While the impact of digital transformation has not yet reached its inflection point, many employees need to acknowledge that their companies' technological evolution moves to the next level based on a growing use of AI. By applying a variety of intelligent algorithms and advanced data analytics solutions, executives leverage the value of the data that is collected in their digitalization initiatives. While this is a natural move from a strategic perspective, the growing use of AI constitutes an additional challenge in many companies' transformation processes. In this regard, some employees are open to adopt the latest AI solutions because they see the opportunities that these technologies offer. Many other employees, by contrast, are reluctant or even scared of these technological evolutions.[1]

Some of this skepticism and fear derives from science fiction scenarios that robots might kill humans and rule the world at some point in the future. Other sources of negative attitudes towards AI can be traced back to employees' fear of losing their jobs because technology may increasingly replace human work. Besides these negative scenarios, many people are fascinated by robots. Thus, attitudes to new technology, especially with regard to intelligent robots, are often ambivalent. In addition, many persons are open to using new technology if they perceive a benefit from it. The growing use of Amazon's Alexa and Apple's Siri assistants is a good example in this regard. Accordingly, many people actually are relatively open to using new technology, including AI, in their private lives and in their own personal environments.

At the same time, however, many people prefer to collaborate with real humans rather than having virtual colleagues without human interaction. Despite some level of openness towards new technology in their environment at home, many employees seem to prefer human colleagues at work. Most probably, however, the emergence of positive or negative attitudes to AI does not only depend on the work or leisure context. Rather, there may be further drivers of employee attitudes towards technology in general and AI in particular. If firms want to benefit from AI applications, employees' attitudes are in fact crucial. However, these attitudes are more complex than expected, which leads to the paradox that the same person may have positive or negative attitudes to AI, depending on the particular situation. So what importance do employees' attitudes have, and is your business really – and are you personally – ready for AI?

Employee attitudes have a major influence on the use of new technologies. A substantial body of research has examined this topic. In particular, the technology acceptance model suggests that various factors, including the usefulness of a new technology – as perceived by employees – affect the decision whether to use it or not.[2] The strong importance of employee attitudes towards new technology may be observed in technology fields that are as diverse as information technology, pharmaceuticals, and machinery. Thus, several factors influence employee attitudes to technology, and these factors are related to the new technology, to the employee, to the human-machine interface as well as other fields. Beyond the general importance of employee attitudes, Not-Invented-Here attitudes are well-known, and they refer to negative attitudes to acquiring technology and knowledge from external sources. As a result, employees are reluctant to collaborate with external partners, and they prefer internal technology development in make-or-buy decisions.[3]

The relevance of Not-Invented-Here attitudes is widely accepted in practice. Over the past decade, these negative attitudes may partly have been reduced because of many companies' evolution from relatively closed to open innovation strategies. Nonetheless, potential positive attitudes to acquiring external knowledge have received less attention, although they may also affect make-or-buy decisions based on the trend towards co-creation. These positive attitudes to external knowledge have been termed Buy-In attitudes, and they describe situations when people think that "the other person's dessert always looks better".[4] Thus, there may be situations where knowledge from external sources is preferred over knowledge from internal sources, for example because the internal knowhow is from colleagues, different business units, or different functional units. Independent of a positive or negative direction, employee attitudes may strongly affect technology acceptance decisions, which in turn impact a company's innovation outcomes and performance. This human side of technological evolution may play a particularly prominent role in the adoption of AI, which often calls for significant changes in the human-machine interface.

The paradox of positive and negative attitudes

The AI initiatives of most companies have focused on increasing efficiency based on replacing human work by means of advanced technology. This substitution of human work only comprises a minor part of the potential competitive advantages because the complementary use of HI and AI will most likely offer more important benefits in the long run than the mere substitution of human work. Nonetheless, this substitution has received major public attention, with speculations as to the number of jobs that may be lost in the transformation. Even in the case of complementarity of HI and AI, executives may face a human-or-machine decision at least for some of the key activities that could be completed by AI or human work in the future. Beyond this human-or-machine decision, there will be a growing relevance of new human-machine interfaces in light of intelligent algorithms and advanced data analytics.

Because of the ambiguity that is associated with changing human-machine interfaces, negative attitudes of employees towards AI may emerge. Drawing on the well-known concept of Not-Invented-Here attitudes, these attitudes are termed No-Human-Interaction (NHI) attitudes, and they are defined as negative attitudes to interactions with AI. When employees exhibit such attitudes, they have a strong preference for personal interactions with humans based on emphasizing emotional intelligence and empathy. Consequently, this type of attitudes typically leads to a limited openness to using AI solutions even in the case of a high usability of these solutions. For example, many people who become aware of Google's Duplex technology, which was presented in 2018, displayed some degree of negative attitudes at the beginning. Based on various functionalities, the technology comprises a personal assistant that is able, for example, to make a reservation by calling a restaurant with a close-to-human voice.

Many people's immediate reaction is that they prefer being called by a human rather than by AI, especially when it is not transparent that it is a computer calling rather than a human. While transparency in communication is important, this is only a minor issue here because many individuals clearly indicate some level of negative attitudes in this respect. However, these negative attitudes are only one side of the coin, because there is a paradox in many persons' attitudes. While being reluctant to take calls from AI, many people agree that they would like their own digital assistant to complete such calls on their behalf. By just changing the perspective from receiving a call or benefitting from having the AI make such a call, many respondents switch from negative to positive attitudes. This is the paradoxical situation of changing attitudes from negative to positive, depending on the particular perspective and situation. Many people prefer collaborating with other humans rather than having AI as virtual colleagues. At the same time, however, they are open to using new technology if it provides them with a benefit.

Drawing on the concept of Buy-In attitudes, these positive attitudes are termed Intelligent-Automation (IA) attitudes, and they are defined as positive attitudes to interactions with AI. Typically, these attitudes increase a person's openness to most types of intelligent automation, while leading to a neutral position concerning personal interactions with humans. Because of emphasizing rational decisions and deemphasizing empathy, people with these attitudes are also open to using advanced technology that has not yet received its final development stage. With a strong focus on convenience and on optimizing everyday processes, respondents with positive attitudes have a relatively balanced view of potential positive and negative consequences of AI, rather than being scared of potential negative effects. Therefore, they also have a somewhat pragmatic approach to data protection and privacy if the solution adds value. In contrast, strongly negative attitudes rather lead to major concerns about data protection and privacy even if the solution adds value. Table 3 provides an overview of key characteristics of these attitudes.

No Human Interaction Attitudes	Intelligent Automation Attitudes
Negative attitudes to interactions with AI	Positive attitudes to interactions with AI
Strong preference for personal interactions with humans	Neutral position concerning personal interactions with humans
Limited openness to using AI solutions even in the case of high usability	Relative openness to using AI solutions which are still in development stage
Strong emphasis on emotional intelligence and empathy	Strong emphasis on rational decisions and limited focus on empathy
Limited focus on convenience, efficiency and optimization	Strong focus on convenience and on optimizing everyday processes
Strong tendency to be afraid of potential negative consequences of AI	Balanced view of potential positive and negative consequences of AI
Strong concerns about data protection and privacy even if AI adds value	Pragmatic approach to data protection and privacy if AI adds value

Table 3: No-Human-Interaction vs. Intelligent-Automation attitudes
(Source: Lichtenthaler, 2019, Journal of Business Strategy[5])

For these characteristics, No-Human-Interaction and Intelligent-Automation attitudes represent the extreme points in a continuum of negative and positive attitudes. Rather than a black-or-white distinction, many persons' attitudes will be somewhere in between these extreme attitudes. Moreover, the paradoxical situation of positive and negative attitudes of the same person may lead to a relative emphasis on negative attitudes towards AI in one situation, whereas positive attitudes may play a more prominent role under other conditions. If a person receives a call from a digital assistant based on the Google Duplex technology, for example, there may be strongly negative attitudes, especially if the digital assistant does not transparently communicate that it is not a human calling. In contrast, if the same person is in a hurry and needs to schedule an appointment for the next day, this person may well exhibit positive attitudes. Beyond a general attitude somewhere between the extremes, there may be a clear focus on either of these attitudes depending on the particular setting.

Both types of employee attitudes may have negative effects on firms' digital transformation initiatives. For example, these attitudes may lead to a suboptimal use of advanced analytics, to higher cost levels relative to competitors, and to problems in innovation, which increasingly draws on digital features and AI. Besides these negative consequences, the need for actively managing employee attitudes is underscored by the paradox that the same employees may exhibit negative or positive attitudes depending on the particular situation. This paradox further complicates firms' digital transformation because a relatively simple training to support a growing application of AI by reducing negative attitudes will not be appropriate in many situations. Rather, a clear understanding of the underlying roots of employee attitudes is essential before deciding on suitable managerial steps.

Roots of attitudes

Employee attitudes may be traced back to multiple roots, which favor the emergence of a specific degree of negative or positive attitudes to AI in a particular situation. These roots fall into the following five categories, which reflect the human-machine interface as well as the dynamic evolution of technologies and typical behaviors in an employee's environment. Figure 8 offers an overview of these selected factors. The first group of factors refers to the human that is involved in the interaction with AI. Here, the affinity towards new technology plays a critical role. Some people are very technology-driven and are typically among the early adopters of a new technology, whereas many others are more reluctant with regard to applying the latest technology, including advanced analytics. Accordingly, an individual's affinity to new technology in general may influence his or her attitudes to AI. An additional key driver is a person's convenience orientation. This orientation reflects to what degree a person is rationally trying to ease and optimize activities rather than being emotionally bound to

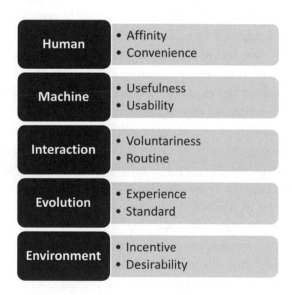

Figure 8: Selected roots of employee attitudes to AI (Source: Lichtenthaler, 2019, Journal of Business Strategy[6])

human interactions. Employees with these characteristics are more likely to exhibit positive attitudes in a given situation because they are aware of the convenience benefits that an active application of AI can offer.

The second group of factors describes key features of an AI application. Thus, it refers to the machine part of the human-machine interface. Here, the usefulness of an application as perceived by the user is a key driver. If a person is convinced that using a particular solution would increase his or her performance, the level of negative attitudes will usually be limited. For example, if an intelligent algorithm of a hotel booking website like booking.com gives you suitable recommendations for your next trip, you will most likely be happy to rely on the underlying technology in order to receive these recommendations. However, if you are living in the US and you regularly receive last-minute hotel offers for the next weekend in Singapore, you are likely to be annoyed by the technology, leading to strongly negative attitudes – because you only stayed in Singapore for one night several years ago and you would never book a weekend trip from the US to Singapore on the strength of a minor hotel discount. Another machine-related key factor is the perceived usability. If a company's employees are convinced that interacting with AI is free from major effort, potential negative attitudes will be reduced.[7] For example, if employees working in a production line realize that the interaction with a robot is very easy and safe, they will be more open to using it.

A third group of factors specifically address the interaction in the human-machine interface. In this regard, it is essential whether an employee voluntarily decides to use AI. Many people who are somewhat reluctant to use new technology happily use auto corrections when typing messages with their smartphone. They are also open to relying on the predictive text suggestions because they may substantially ease the writing process, especially for complex words. Although many such people are somewhat skeptical with regard to data collection and self-learning mechanisms of the software, these potential negative attitudes do not fully materialize because the persons freely choose to rely on this technology. Another key factor is whether the human-machine interaction is a routine activity. Many people are open to using automatic self-checkout in their ordinary supermarket shopping because it is a regular task that they need to get done. In contrast, they would favor a personal interaction with a salesperson when they are shopping for regional souvenirs in their summer vacation. Routine interactions favor the emergence of positive rather than negative attitudes.

The fourth group of factors captures the dynamic evolution of behaviors over time. If an employee has hardly any prior experience using AI, the emergence of negative attitudes is quite likely. With an increasing exposure to AI, however, these negative attitudes may be reduced. Even if a person is still reluctant to use an automatic self-checkout in a supermarket today, the same person may be more open to do so after trying this check-out method several times. This change of behaviors would be similar to cash withdrawal from a counter, which has been largely replaced by ATMs. This path-dependent evolution is typical for employee attitudes towards new technology. If an activity involving advanced analytics becomes standard, e. g. complex analyses of radiology results, negative attitudes will be less relevant. Even if experience has not been accumulated personally, the emergence of new standards will increase most employees' openness towards using AI. Thus, the behaviors of individuals will likely change over time along with changes in the underlying attitudes. Like the dynamic understanding of the scope of AI, employee attitudes towards AI solutions will also evolve over time.

Finally, the fifth group of factors refers to a person's environment, which includes the work environment inside an organization as well as the external environment outside the organization. With regard to the internal organizational environment, a key factor are incentives, which can shape an employee's attitudes. Executives may rely on monetary and non-monetary incentives for strengthening the use of advanced technology among their employees. Even people that are relatively reluctant to use AI may become more open towards actively using a particular solution if they highly value the monetary or non-monetary incentives. As such, incentives may be helpful at least in the transition phase towards a stronger use of AI. Beyond the internal environment, the social desirability of relying on AI solutions may drive the emergence of positive or negative attitudes. While face recognition systems based on biometric AI are relatively well accepted in some countries, people from other cultures, such as Germany, are noticeably reluctant to agree to a broader use of this particular technology. Accordingly, the environment has a major effect on the emergence and articulation of particular employee attitudes towards AI.

Managing the paradox

Jointly, the five groups of factors help to describe the development of positive or negative attitudes to AI in particular situations. The five categories represent key categories of factors shaping the emergence of particular employee attitudes towards AI. However, this list of factors is not exhaustive, and there are other relevant factors in the five groups and beyond. Nonetheless, these five categories are important for understanding the variety of roots of employees' attitudes towards AI. Therefore, executives who plan to support the adoption of AI in their organizations by means of influencing the attitudes of their employees need to proceed carefully. In light of the complexity of employee attitudes towards AI and their underlying roots, the suitable design of organizational interventions is more difficult than most executives initially assume. The dynamic nature of employee attitudes and behaviors, which may substantially change over time, further complicates the assessment and transformation of employee attitudes to AI.

Overall, the new concepts of No-Human-Interaction and Intelligent-Automation attitudes deepen the understanding of companies' success and problems in implementing advanced data analytics. Moreover, the paradox of negative and positive attitudes among the same employees helps to reconcile partly diverging findings in extant studies about the perception of the opportunities and risks of AI. At the present evolutionary stage, positive attitudes may play a role in some specific situations, but in most business contexts negative attitudes prevail. Consequently, many executives face the challenge of shifting employee attitudes towards neutral or positive attitudes. The groups of factors influencing the emergence of negative or positive attitudes also offer important starting points for actively managing these attitudes. With regard to the human factors, executives may place great emphasis on attitudes to new technology in the hiring process of employees, especially for those departments where a strong interaction with AI is required. In addition, executives may assign the role of gatekeepers to selected employees, who formally or informally support a balanced use of intelligent solutions in the organization. By championing the use of AI, these gatekeepers may become key influencers for other employees.

Regarding the machine-related factors, executives need to put a strong emphasis on the excellent usability of new applications. In addition, a highly useful initial application may give a major impulse to employees and may lead to enthusiasm for this technological change. Concerning the interaction-related factors, executives need to openly communicate the scope and direction of AI initiatives. A high level of transparency is particularly important when new applications affect the HR department. With regard to the experience factors, ample opportunities for testing new applications may strongly contribute to the acceptance of these technologies. Furthermore, some quick wins with the first applications may lead to a self-reinforcing cycle towards an organizational climate that favors the adoption of AI. With respect to the factors in employees' environment, executives may design incentive schemes that consider the successful adoption of AI. In addition, organizational structures may support implementation. For instance, new applications may be implemented in selected units before rolling them out in the entire organization.

While negative attitudes to AI may currently be observed in many situations, there will be a shift towards more positive attitudes in the future. This expected evolution may well ease the implementation of new applications. At the same time, however, the coexistence of No-Human-Interaction and Intelligent-Automation attitudes may strengthen the paradox of positive and negative attitudes emerging in the same group of employees depending on the particular situation. Moreover, the growing relevance of positive attitudes in practice may complicate an active management of employee attitudes because suitable interventions will strongly depend on the particular situation and context. With a growing competitive relevance, however, unprofessional interactions with AI may have serious negative consequences on company performance. Thus, businesses do not have an alternative to addressing employee attitudes because the interface of human and artificial intelligence will be an important driver of future competitive advantage.

Chapter 12

The SMART leadership framework

New times call for new management and leadership approaches, and they further call for reconsidering the role of HR departments in companies. The discussions in the previous chapters have shown that a growing use of AI usually leads to a more important role of complex business ecosystems, which go beyond a company's traditional buyer-supplier relationships in a well-established industry context. Moreover, the emergence of positive or negative attitudes among many companies' employees leads to new challenges for management at different hierarchical levels. Consequently, executives not only need to reconsider strategies, processes, and organizational structures. Rather, they need to question established leadership processes and management routines which may also reshape the role of the HR department in companies. Accordingly, transforming a company's intelligence architecture to embody a growing role of AI may well go along with transforming the entire management and leadership procedures in the organization.[1]

In fact, many firms have started to transform their business activities in several ways, and these transformations will continue over the next years. The variety of these transformations indicates that the impact of AI and changing intelligence architectures extends to multiple business activities beyond advanced data analytics and new algorithms. Accordingly, companies currently innovate their management approaches rather than only focusing on new products, processes, services, or business models, which are enabled by integrated intelligence. A management innovation refers to the invention and implementation of a novel management practice, technique, process, or leadership style.[2] As such, it involves a change in the form, state, or quality of a company's management activities. Many organizations have recently introduced several management innovations, which have substantially changed their management and leadership approaches. Beyond AI, for example, many companies put a stronger emphasis on achieving a dynamic competitive advantage by continuously innovating their products. In the past, companies placed relatively more emphasis on securing their current competitive position rather than being open to potentially cannibalizing their own products by continuously offering new models and solutions.

Ultimately, the variety of environmental trends may help adaptable companies thrive, whereas others will face severe problems. Currently, many businesses struggle to profit from these trends, which are partly based on new technological advances and partly on the evolution of markets and societies. Thus, the trends comprise fundamental technological, economic, and societal evolutions that lead to new management principles. Examples of important technological trends – beyond AI – which drive new leadership approaches are social networks and the convergence of multiple technology fields, for instance autonomous and connected mobility in the cars of the future. An example of major economic trends is the growing innovative power of certain countries, such as China. Companies from these countries become global competitors, and Western companies adapt their management principles in reaction to these developments. Examples of societal trends encouraging new management approaches are the growing income levels in several developing countries, which open up new opportunities for firms based on suitable managerial approaches.

Together, these trends challenge many conventional management guidelines, leadership principles, and strategy frameworks, because several common approaches do not seem to be applicable under the new conditions. For instance, AI enables completely new solutions in the field of people analytics, and these solutions provide various new opportunities in the context of managing human resources, but also new challenges with regard to the human-machine interface. An example beyond the core topic of AI is the conventional advice to focus on developing internal core competencies inside the organization. Somewhat in contrast with this suggestion, many companies now consider their ecosystem of external partnerships with other firms as a critical core competence. Therefore, new leadership approaches are needed to respond to these developments and to integrate the logic of business transformations in relatively dispersed fields, including product development, HR management, and strategic planning.

Indeed, many companies have acknowledged the relevance of these transformations, but they are unable to react accordingly based on established leadership principles. In fact, conventional management tools may limit a company's transformation towards an intelligence-based organization. In particular, new leadership approaches in the context of AI need to go beyond what traditionally is considered as the leadership domain. Rather than merely focusing on a specific leader-follower relationship, there are broader leadership challenges in the context of AI in order to enable a successful transformation towards integrated intelligence architectures comprising AI and HI. As such, these leadership challenges also include strategic, processual, organizational, and cultural aspects. Triggered by several contributing factors, these trends will result in a new approach to management and leadership, which is called 'SMART leadership'. This chapter shows how companies can reap the benefits from these trends and management innovations by applying the principles of SMART leadership.

SMART leadership principles

In response to the growing relevance of AI and multiple related evolutions, executives can rely on the new framework of SMART leadership, which comprises five major principles. These principles indicate that essential leadership guidelines have been transformed. Relative to prior approaches, management has become increasingly SMART, i.e. situational, mutual, analytical, relational, and transformational (Figure 9). Each of these principles covers one of the central leadership and management dimensions that have recently been affected by a new logic in the context of AI and digitalization. The five principles indicate that the transformations towards integrated intelligence architectures affect multiple facets of leadership, which challenge conventional management wisdom. Taken together, these principles provide the basis for the SMART leadership framework, which may serve as an initial step towards an up-to-date picture and realistic guideline for today's leadership and management in many organizations. In the following, each of the five principles is addressed. Real-life examples of selected companies are given, and many other firms' managerial challenges in applying and profiting from these principles are described.

The first principle of the SMART leadership framework refers to the tendency that leadership becomes increasingly situational. The basic assumption follows earlier leadership approaches, which suggest that there is not one single best approach to leadership. However, the focus here is not on adapting leadership approaches to an employee's performance readiness or maturity level.[4] Rather, large companies can fuel their growth by facilitating and encouraging flexible leadership approaches to stimulate

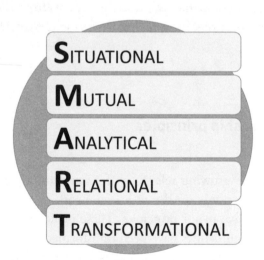

Figure 9: SMART leadership principles
(Source: partly adapted from Lichtenthaler, 2016, Journal of Business Strategy[3])

innovation and to overcome an excessive focus on efficiency. In start-up teams, the founders often share critical competencies, and large firms now attempt to imitate these processes at large scale. In this regard, executives tend to deemphasize consistent and formalized leadership that would enable clear and predictable leadership approaches to a particular situation. Rather, many leaders perceive their companies to be in a constant state of emergency, which calls for flexible managerial responses. As such, companies rely on situational leadership, which enables flexible actions in particular situations to ensure that their large and established organizations remain sufficiently agile. Besides implementing more entrepreneurial behaviors in everyday management processes and techniques, large established companies further rely on independent start-up teams in a separate location to foster situational leadership and the development of radically new ideas that could threaten their established products and business models. An excellent example is the successful transformation of the German software supplier SAP, which has focused on new leadership approaches for innovation and entrepreneurship to stimulate its growth and to enhance its product development.

By emphasizing situational leadership approaches that facilitate flexibility and entrepreneurial spirit, companies attempt to overcome the primary focus on established processes and management routines that might limit new ideas and creativity. As such, many companies complement established processes with relatively independent activities. Consequently, they do not question the traditional strategy suggestion to focus on efficiency for achieving economies of scale and scope. Based on a situational approach, however, companies attempt to overcome the negative effects of size and bureaucracy in established organizations by additionally pursuing more flexible activities, which are sometimes labelled 'intrapreneurship' rather than entrepreneurship to indicate their internal character. By relying on situational leadership approaches in the context of a growing use of AI, businesses also try to respond to paradoxical situations like the emergence of negative or positive attitudes to AI among their employees. Thus, large firms pursue situational leadership and lean operations to combine the benefits of flexible and adaptive start-ups in particular situations with the efficiency gains of established organizations. As such, they overcome many large companies' traditional focus on primarily enhancing efficiency based on relatively strict leadership guidelines.

The second principle of the SMART leadership framework refers to the tendency that leadership is becoming increasingly mutual and multifaceted. Many organizations today pursue a participatory leadership approach, which acknowledges the benefits of strongly involving the leader and the followers to enable comprehensive and diverse intelligence architectures. As such, many executives take an integrative perspective, and they apply a shared leadership logic in their organizations. By encouraging project responsibility of diverse members in agile project teams, many firms attempt to achieve an overall optimum rather than excessively focusing on optimizing a few selected activities. Thus, companies acknowledge the synergies among multiple individual human intelligences with AI, including experts from multiple functional departments, multiple development teams, and so on. Moreover, companies further share knowledge on a global scale, thus going beyond a separate optimization of individual facets. An example is the Chilean airline LATAM, which has implemented relatively mutual leadership approaches in order to manage three diverse business models and to maximize its overall performance.[5]

By adopting a mutual leadership approach, many companies are starting to go beyond traditional management recommendations. For example, companies' leadership and organizational solutions tend to become increasingly participatory, going beyond the top-down implementation of formalized strategies. In addition, companies now implement a stronger interface management to optimize interactions among multiple functional departments, such as marketing or R&D, which often developed separately with different functional cultures in a single company. As such, leadership is increasingly shared in dispersed teams based on team members' particular personal characteristics. Part of this mutual approach is the development of truly global strategies in all aspects of business in order to overcome the potential limitations of a strong home country focus and to fully leverage the multiple facets of global organizations. While different organizational units will always play a central role in most firms, many companies now rely on stronger coordinating mechanisms to achieve a global rather than local optimum based on mutual leadership.

The third principle of the SMART leadership framework refers to the tendency of leadership to become increasingly analytical. Beyond the mere implementation of advanced analytics and smart algorithms, companies rely on new management and leadership techniques. On this basis, executives attempt to arrive at personalized leadership approaches. For example, the growing use of people analytics enables more customized leadership styles in response to the specific leader-follower relationship. In addition, executives rely on evidence from data analytics and empirical studies to optimize their internal managerial solutions by drawing on data and empirical evidence as a basis for decision-making. Thus, companies attempt to apply scientific methods to evaluating practice. Furthermore, businesses rely on AI to leverage the power of big data analytics based on the data that they collect as a result of digital transformation initiatives. Here, Google is an outstanding example, which has used its AI capabilities, data processing power, and intelligence-based leadership approaches to optimize its search engine and to enter completely new fields, such as the health industry, by conducting research and development based on data processing methods.[6]

In doing so companies are overcoming a number of established leadership principles. Many of these principles were developed when the data-based understanding of personal traits and behaviors was not available to its current degree. Moreover, AI was hardly used at that time in most companies. Consequently, they focused on traditional leadership approaches with a high importance accorded to subjective gut feelings of leaders with respect to their followers. In contrast, leadership did not have a major link to personalized data and empirical research. Today, however, companies have many new opportunities based on analytical management techniques for leadership, HR management, and many other topics. These tools and methods often rely on AI to analyze large volumes of data from multiple sources to allow for optimizing a company's existing business as well as moving into completely new fields by leveraging existing competencies. Beyond pure leadership, traditional management recommendations concerning related diversification need to be extended to incorporate new dimensions of relatedness, such as data analytics and advanced algorithms.

The fourth dimension of the SMART leadership framework refers to the tendency of management to become increasingly relational. Thus, companies emphasize a variety of leader and follower relationships in the context of complex intelligence architectures. These intelligence architectures include strong relations and networks with other organizations in business ecosystems instead of being largely focused on their particular organization. Executives have realized that even large companies often lack critical resources, and they need leadership principles to capture the value of shared resources, partly in contrast with established management guidelines. For instance, many companies face a growing convergence of multiple technology fields, and they are unable to master all technological changes by means of internal developments. Consequently, they rely on resource sharing and co-creation processes, which involve active collaborations with external partners. These new approaches have led to large portfolios of external alliances and networks. As such, the management of these relations has become a central competence for many organizations. Good examples are many telecommunications providers, such as AT&T, which orchestrate solutions offered by multiple partner firms.

This relational understanding of leadership contrasts with many conventional suggestions concerning competitive advantage. External collaborations have long played an important role. In a similar vein, the optimization of the entire value chain involving a company's suppliers and customers has long been considered critical for competitive advantage. What has changed, though, is the understanding that a company alone may outperform many others in terms of its products, processes, and solutions without achieving a competitive advantage because of insufficient relational resources. In light of a growing role of AI, competitive advantage may reside in business ecosystems with complementary products and services. Under such conditions, firms may have to closely collaborate with direct competitors. Moreover, they may collaborate with other firms in one particular regional market, whereas they are fierce competitors in other markets. Thus, firms need to increasingly aim at achieving a relational advantage rather than a traditional competitive advantage for their single organization. Accordingly, leadership also needs to go beyond individual leadership settings in the context of a single company's activities.

Finally, the fifth dimension of the SMART leadership framework refers to the tendency that management becomes increasingly transformational. As such, executives acknowledge that their companies often can only achieve temporal competitive advantages rather than continuous long-term advantages. In many markets, multiple companies will have some degree of competitive advantage over time, and this understanding partially contrasts with traditional management guidelines. Consequently, companies increasingly rely on transformational management principles to encourage agility. Beyond the distinction of transformational and transactional leadership[7], companies focus on regular strategic renewal based on accepting the limited possibilities to retain established advantages over long periods of time. Thus, they put a stronger emphasis on experimentation to renew and to revive their business activities and business models. Accordingly, organizational transformation becomes a central leadership capability for ensuring long-term success and survival. This principle is exemplified by Amazon's continuous transformation and extension of its business from a bookseller to cloud computing and beyond.

These new management approaches challenge many conventional leadership recommendations. Of course, the renewal of organizations was always necessary, but it has gained particular importance in the context of a more active of AI, more dynamic environments, and more intense competition. The understanding of temporal advantages and continuous renewal based on an adaptable intelligence architecture challenges the traditional focus on long-term strategic planning. Long-term strategies need to be complemented by emerging strategies, which continuously renew and reshape a firm's strategic direction. Organizations need to dynamically adapt their behaviors, leadership principles, and strategic options in order to proactively pursue their strategies and to reactively respond to sudden developments, which happen regularly. Consequently, executives need to focus on transformational approaches in order to overcome the primarily static emphasis on long-term business and corporate strategies to allow for agile leadership and dynamic competitive advantages.

Implementing SMART leadership

The importance of the five principles of SMART leadership continues to grow because of the stronger role of AI and a variety of environmental trends, which contribute to an increasingly SMART approach to leadership and management. Hence, firms developing new management principles continue to build on a new logic of leadership. Accordingly, the underlying trends and drivers strengthen five different management principles, which are unified by their focus on new leadership and which involve substantial management innovations. The SMART leadership framework acknowledges the relevance of these trends and helps companies to reap their particular benefits. As such, it contrasts with several established recommendations for managing people and organizations (Table 4). The distinction of conventional and SMART leadership approaches is not a clear-cut separation but rather a continuum with many organizations located between the two extremes for some of the dimensions. Nonetheless, there is a tendency towards SMART leadership principles in many organizations.

Dimensions	Conventional leadership	SMART leadership
Situational	Primary focus on consistent leadership and established management routines, emphasizing efficiency and optimization	Focus on flexible leadership approaches, innovation, intrapreneurship and independent startup teams in large firms
Mutual	Top-down leadership, emphasizing hierarchy and relatively strict managerial roles in the organization	Participatory leadership, high importance of expert roles, shared leadership and project responsibility in agile teams
Analytical	Limited link to data and empirical analyses in leadership approaches, high importance of subjective gut feelings	Strong use of people analytics and further advanced data analytics to enable and to enhance personalized leadership approaches

Dimensions	Conventional leadership	SMART leadership
Relational	Primary focus on individual leadership settings in the context of a single firm's strategy and competitive advantage	Variety of leader and follower relationships in the context of complex intelligence architectures across eco-system partners
Transfor-mational	Leadership focus on long-term strategies and planning to achieve a competitive advantage over long periods	Leadership focus on agility and temporal competitive advantages, emphasis on strategic renewal and organizational transformation

Table 4: Conventional leadership vs. SMART leadership
(Source: partly adapted from Lichtenthaler, 2016,
Journal of Business Strategy[8])

Overall, the five principles of the SMART leadership framework may substantially change businesses' approach to management and governance. Consequently, they constitute the basis for remarkable management innovations. Many companies consider each of the five dimensions an important step towards enhancing their management and leadership approaches. Thus, the SMART leadership principles obviously pay off for a variety of firms. They are relevant to various types of firms and other organizations. Although the examples that have been given above focus on large companies from selected sectors, such as airlines and electronics, the results are also applicable to relatively small companies and to companies from other industries, such as banking, chemicals, construction, and machinery. Based on the growing relevance of AI and of other environmental trends, the SMART leadership principles are particularly important for companies in dynamic and complex settings.

Despite the benefits of some pioneering companies, many others are not successful in implementing SMART leadership principles, and the actual benefits often do not live up to expectations. Some of the implementation challenges may derive from companies' focus on a few specific changes in a relatively isolated way without acknowledging the fundamental character of changing management principles. For instance, it is a major transition from a strategic focus on established processes and efficiency gains towards an entrepreneurial culture and innovation with more situational leadership. By the same token, it requires major changes to move from a relatively top-down leadership with an emphasis on hierarchy to mutual leadership with a high importance of expert roles in agile projects. Taking into account the different dimensions of the SMART leadership framework may help managers understand the complex nature of the changes, and it may ease the transformation processes.

By considering the different dimensions of the SMART leadership framework, firms may acknowledge potential positive and negative synergies and interdependencies among the five principles. For example, there is a positive relation between the 'situational' and 'transformational' dimensions. If companies move towards a more flexible and entrepreneurial culture based on situational leadership, this will typically also allow for a more dynamic approach based on transformational leadership. Executives have to balance adaptability based on transformational and situational leadership on the one hand with efficiency based on established routines and conventional leadership on the other. This balance depends on a company's particular strategy and environment, and SMART leadership principles contribute to achieving such balance. For instance, a relational approach with large external networks and an analytical approach considering advanced analytics of all available data allow for pursuing adaptability and efficiency in a balanced way.

Concerning potential negative interdependencies among the five principles, there may be some tensions – at least at first glance – between the dimensions 'analytical' and 'mutual'. If management becomes increasingly analytical, it may appear to be challenging to take a participatory perspective based on mutual leadership. However, SMART leadership actually allows for combining and integrating both dimensions. If leadership is more analytical, managers will have more data and information to take well-informed decisions, and the results of people analytics solutions may be shared or have to be shared with the particular employees. Consequently, the decision preparation may become more complex, but it may actually ease the development of a mutual and multifaceted approach –

under the condition that organizations are able to cope with the complexity based on SMART leadership processes. In a similar vein, several other potential tensions may be mitigated by pursuing the underlying logic of new leadership in light of a growing importance of AI and by implementing the SMART leadership framework.

In this regard, executives may follow a step-by-step approach to changing their organizations' management principles in order to facilitate the implementation of SMART leadership and to profit from the variety of environmental trends driving the need for management innovations. Pursuing the following five-step procedure does not detail all necessary activities, but it presents an overview of the most critical activities, and it applies to implementing SMART leadership principles in a variety of organizations. First, executives need to analyze the relevant environmental trends to evaluate the need for changing their companies' management principles. Second, managers have to examine the necessary changes for each of the five principles of the SMART leadership framework. Third, companies have to acknowledge the interdependencies among the five principles in order to plan the overall changes for the organization. Fourth, executives implement the changes by adapting their companies' leadership and management principles. Here, the actual changes of the leadership styles, management tools, and procedures take place. Fifth and finally, executives have to ensure a regular control and potential adaptation of the leadership principles.

Based on this step-by-step procedure, companies may effectively benefit from SMART leadership principles. This procedure shows how firms may overcome the substantial managerial challenges that many other companies experience in implementing these new leadership and management principles. Following the generic five-step procedure eases the implementation process, but it needs to be detailed and tailored to the particular situation and challenges of each organization. The implementation steps further show how companies can enhance their performance based on new leadership principles. Many companies advance towards the management innovations that go along with SMART leadership in terms of several if not all of the five principles. This evolution can be observed despite the severe implementation challenges of many companies. Taken together, these observations underscore the relevance of SMART leadership. If companies aim at strengthening their leadership and management practices in the future, they may well have to consider SMART leadership styles. Exclusively following the conventional leadership approaches might not be an option anymore because it may well be insufficient for achieving superior performance in the context of a growing importance of AI. As many businesses still struggle with succeeding in an intelligence-based context, the five-step procedure provides an immediate starting point for managers in enhancing their likelihood of success by applying SMART leadership principles.

Part E
Implementation

Chapter 13
Corporate initiatives and moving from HR to HAIR

Many large companies actively use multiple AI solutions. While some companies are quite successful, the AI activities of many others have not yet met the high initial expectations. Of course, AI initiatives can fail for a variety of reasons, and some of the typical pitfalls as well as ways to avoid them are discussed in the last chapter of this book. However, one key issue needs to be highlighted here because it affects the very start of AI initiatives in companies. Many companies have a relatively bad start into using AI simply because of the way they set up – or do not set up – their AI activities. In particular, this topic boils down to the issue of whether AI activities are implemented in an ad-hoc way with some isolated applications in one or more parts of the organization or whether there is a more coherent corporate-level initiative for the AI activities. In many situations, it is reasonable to start with some AI activities, but typically these activities need to be complemented by a more systematic and strategic approach from a corporate perspective.

This is not to say that it would always be suitable to develop a relatively formalized corporate-level strategy for AI before starting with any operational AI implementation. Rather, the field of AI is so dynamic that experimentation and flexibility are essential to ease implementation and to enhance the probabilities of success. In many large companies, however, some stand-alone AI activities have emerged in different organizational units. While this approach is helpful to take the first steps and to see what is currently possible or not, it is usually not enough for fully leveraging the potential benefits of AI implementation. This approach will often be insufficient for exploiting AI in terms of efficiency and optimization, but it is particularly insufficient for sparking innovation and growth based on AI. To achieve these benefits, companies typically need to closely align their AI initiatives with other activities, such as product development. Merely implementing stand-alone AI solutions will not be enough for encouraging creativity and for achieving a close interplay of AI and HI in order to generate new revenue streams.

Of course, large organizations may succeed in profiting from their AI activities without establishing some overarching corporate AI strategy. Even in those cases, however, there will usually be some blank spots in the companies' AI landscape, and a corporate perspective may help to identify the opportunities that have remained unrealized so far. In particular, a comprehensive perspective on a company's AI activities is helpful for enabling an integrated intelligence architecture that is more than the sum of the different types of AI and HI in the organization. A relatively isolated implementation of new AI solutions is possible, but their close integration in a firm's intelligence architecture will be hardly possible without a comprehensive company-level perspective. In fact, the idea of achieving an intelligence-based competitive advantage by means of Intelligence^x – comprising various types of AI and HI as well as meta-intelligence – requires an integrated perspective on all AI activities in the organization and beyond.

Managing corporate AI initiatives

Executives should be open to experiment with selected AI solutions as stand-alone applications in different parts of the company. Beyond these individual projects, however, it is necessary to take a portfolio perspective on the entire set of ongoing AI projects. This AI project portfolio perspective is a minimum requirement because usually it is even better to consider the entire portfolio of digital innovation projects beyond a mere focus on AI. Accordingly, companies need to manage the entire list of active AI projects in the context of all digital innovation and transformation projects. On this basis, executives can ensure that they manage the right AI projects rather than just managing AI projects in the right way. While correctly managing projects is possible by taking a single project perspective, selecting the right projects requires a portfolio perspective on a company's digital innovation and AI projects. This portfolio perspective is further key for aligning a company's AI projects with the HI of its internal experts in order to advance towards an integrated intelligence architecture.[1]

Thus, a company's project portfolio needs to be actively managed by taking decisions about continuing, stopping, redirecting, or speeding up projects, including the relevant budgeting decisions. On this basis, companies may further achieve synergies among the variety of projects. For example, companies may have to combine a machine learning algorithm with natural language processing and several other AI solutions as well as different types of HI in order to fully leverage the benefits of each solution. While the implementation of each AI solution is often managed in a separate project, the portfolio perspective enables the exploitation of positive synergies while avoiding negative synergies among these projects. Interestingly, this project portfolio perspective is relatively well established in many companies' innovation management and project management activities, but it is largely neglected so far for AI. Consequently, many AI activities remain isolated initiatives that do not meet the initial expectations. To avoid at least this particular type of failure in implementing AI, digital innovation portfolio management is an important means.

The established innovation portfolio management in companies typically pursues the following goals. First, companies maximize the portfolio's value by selecting the financially most promising projects. Second, executives need to ensure a close alignment between their firm's strategy and the project portfolio. Third, managers have to support and select the right number of projects relative to the available resources and budget. Fourth and finally, companies need to find some balance between different types of projects, such as radical and incremental projects. Beyond these traditional goals, AI initiatives call for considering additional goals in each of these four dimensions (Figure 10). Concerning the first dimension of value, executives need to consider whether AI initiatives generate new revenue streams beyond providing efficiency gains. Regarding the second dimension of strategy, companies need to develop a convincing storyline for their intelligence-based future competitiveness. With respect to the third dimension of resources, AI may have a varying impact on the digital and organizational transformation of firms. Concerning the fourth dimension of balance, AI activities should have some link to a company's core business rather than focusing on largely isolated solutions, which could be easily imitated by competitors.

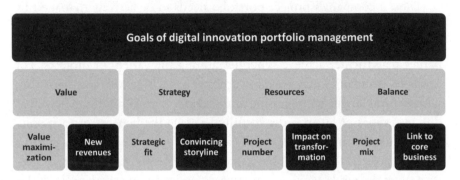

Figure 10: Goals of digital innovation portfolio management (Source: Lichtenthaler, 2019, Zeitschrift Führung + Organisation[2])

To illustrate these different dimensions of digital innovation portfolio management, just consider Amazon's patent for anticipatory shipping. This is not a new story because the patent was already granted in 2013, and it has been addressed in numerous previous publications and the media.[3] Nonetheless, it is an excellent example, and it shows how far the leading companies already envisioned new business models based on AI several years ago. Essentially, anticipatory shipping refers to a situation when Amazon already ships some products because it expects customers to shop these products in the near future based on advanced analytics of the available customer data, customer behavior, and previous touchpoints of the customer with regard to the particular product. This approach would enable Amazon to send you what you want even before you have clearly articulated that you actually want to have it by clicking the buy button. Rather than waiting until you click the button, Amazon is perfectly prepared, and the product is already on the way.

There are several implementation challenges, of course. For example, the accuracy of predictions needs to be high in order to avoid a strong increase in logistics costs. However, this AI solution will enable a substantial transformation of the business model from 'shop & ship' to 'ship & shop'. To implement the solution, several digital and non-digital innovations need to be combined with AI. In the end, the solution contributes to the four goals of portfolio management. First, it enables Amazon to generate new revenues. Second, it strengthens the corporation's storyline for an intelligence-based future business. Third, it has a major impact on the transformation of the entire business beyond AI. Fourth, it has a strong link to Amazon's core business because it changes and potentially extends this core business. Accordingly, the four goals of managing a digital innovation portfolio underscore why this is a promising project. At the same time, this example illustrates the relevance and benefits of establishing a portfolio management that coordinates the entire list of a company's ongoing AI activities in the broader context of all digital innovation projects.

Accordingly, companies should continue to experiment with individual AI solutions in an agile way. In addition, however, a company-level portfolio perspective on AI projects will usually pay off because it helps to achieve an integrated intelligence architecture and to identify blank spots in this architecture in terms of particular types of AI and HI. Moreover, digital innovation portfolio management eases the development of a convincing storyline for a company's intelligence-based future. A convincing storyline is equally relevant internally and externally. Internally, it provides strategic direction for AI decisions and investments. Externally, it helps to convince customers and further stakeholders that a company's products, services, and solutions will be state-of-the-art in an intelligence-based competitive arena. Adopting a corporate-level perspective rather than managing individual AI projects in an isolated way constitutes an important success factor in starting AI activities and in integrating these activities in a firm's intelligence architecture.

The role of the C-suite

Beyond the need for agile experimentation with multiple AI solutions, a company-level coordination of AI activities is helpful. If we accept this need for company-level coordination, this immediately leads to several other questions. Who ought to oversee this company-level coordination? Is it helpful to establish a dedicated unit for orchestrating the AI activities? What is the role of the C-suite? Do companies need a Chief Artificial Intelligence Officer? What role does the Chief Digital Officer have with regard to AI? What contributions may the Chief Technology Officer or Chief Information Officer provide? It is difficult to give a general answer to many of these and related questions because they strongly depend on a company's particular situation and especially on the historical evolution of the roles and responsibilities within the organization. Thus, company-specific responses and managerial solutions are needed, but one overall recommendation can be given: the C-suite needs to be actively involved.

Apart from exceptional situations, C-level executives will not personally implement particular AI solutions. However, the business impact and potentially disruptive character of AI are so strong that it deserves close attention from the Chief Executive Officer and other top executives. In this regard, a firm's top executives play a particularly prominent role in ensuring that a firm is not only aiming for intelligent leadership, but also tries to achieve intelligence leadership. Intelligent leadership primarily refers to clever leadership in light of a growing role of AI. By contrast, intelligence leadership means that a company aims at being a leader in terms of intelligence relative to its competitors. In addition, intelligence leadership means that a company's executives need to extend their leadership roles towards managing their intelligence architecture with regard to AI and HI. Thus, intelligence leadership goes well beyond intelligent leadership, which could already be achieved by fulfilling traditional leadership roles in a clever way.

Besides the overall need for intelligence leadership and the involvement of C-level executives, the increasing role of AI illustrates that lifelong learning is needed at all hierarchical levels. The growing importance of AI also calls for some threshold knowledge about data analytics and smart algorithms among the top executives. Even if these individuals do not need to become experts in AI technology, they need some basic insights into the potential opportunities and implementation challenges of AI. In particular, they need some understanding about the potential transformation of business models, organizations, and industries beyond the relatively isolated application of particular AI solutions in specific business processes in selected parts of the organization. The opportunities and threats of AI can be largely traced back to technological advances, but the key insights and knowledge for the top executives refer to the market, business, and organizational consequences rather than to the technological details.

While it is helpful for all top executives to accumulate some AI expertise, the implementation of particular AI solutions will be a core task for some top executives. Here, the Chief Technology Officer may play a major role, but that person is often not perfectly prepared for managing an AI initiative. While the implementation of AI usually brings considerable technological challenges, it is usually far from a company's core fields of technology. For instance, a company may continue to build on its core technological strength in mechanical engineering, which is quite different from AI technologies. In a similar vein, the Chief Information Officer may play an important role. However, this person often does not focus on product-related information technology. Consequently, some AI solutions, such as particular machine learning algorithms, may be directly related to a company's established IT applications. Nonetheless, the Chief Information Officer usually does not emphasize the interplay of AI and HI. In a similar vein, the Chief Information Officer's role typically does not comprise the development of new business models based on AI.

To overcome this limited emphasis of existing top management roles, many companies have established the position of a Chief Digital Officer in recent years. The key role of this person is managing a company's digital transformation by highlighting the urgent need for change and by enabling the transformation processes. As such, the Chief Digital Officer does not operationally manage all digital transformation activities. Rather, this person is a promoter and orchestrator of the digitalization initiatives. Moreover, establishing the role of a Chief Digital Officer may be a major signal, internally and externally. In particular, it shows a firm's internal employees and external stakeholders that the company is putting high strategic priority to its digital transformation initiative. In particular, the Chief Digital Officer has a key role in the implementation of product-related IT solutions and new data-based business activities beyond using digital solutions for internal process improvements and efficiency increases.

On this basis, the Chief Digital Officer has provided an important contribution in many, though not in all, companies. In addition, some firms have considered the Chief Digital Officer only as a temporary position from the beginning, and they think about abolishing this role as soon as some major milestones have been reached in their digital transformation processes. However, the Chief Digital Officer may also play an important role with regard to the implementation of AI solutions because this person is already involved in product-related IT solutions and data-based business models. These activities are among the core fields where advanced analytics and smart algorithms can unfold their full potential. Accordingly, it is a relatively natural move to assign some of the AI related tasks to the Chief Digital Officer, whereas other AI applications may be coordinated by the Chief Information Officer, e. g. the use of AI to ease internal managerial processes. Independent of the influence of a Chief Digital Officer, the Chief Executive Officer needs to be fully committed to the digital transformation activities and support the Chief Digital Officer.

In this context, companies may also think about establishing the dedicated role of a Chief Artificial Intelligence Officer. In fact, some large technology companies have already assigned this role, but this person is not necessarily a full member of the top executive team. Notwithstanding the exact hierarchical level, a dedicated executive and department for coordinating the AI activities offers several advantages. However, the success of a firm's AI initiatives will usually not depend on whether a person has the title of the Chief Artificial Intelligence Officer or whether the responsibilities of a Chief Digital Officer are extended to AI. Typically, it is more important that there is a high-ranking person who has the support from the top, including the Chief Executive Officer and the other members of the top executive team. On this basis, the person may play a major role in turning an organization's AI activities into a success, which is not limited to isolated applications of some advanced algorithms.

Rather, the person overseeing the AI activities will be the central contact and coordination hub for all AI activities. Thus, this person enables intelligence and organizational learning about AI beyond individual learning and intelligence. In particular, the person may help to educate the top executives and to elevate their relevant knowledge about AI. On this basis, a dedicated AI executive may contribute to using AI for developing innovative solutions and generating new revenues rather than focusing exclusively on strengthening internal efficiency. Since data analytics may offer completely new business opportunities, a dedicated executive can also be considered the equivalent to the leaders of established business lines. Moreover, this person can further manage the relationships to universities and other research institutions with regard to AI. Similar to a Chief Digital Officer, a dedicated AI role may have a strong signaling effect, internally and externally. As such, a company can put further emphasis on developing a convincing storyline for its success in future intelligence-based markets. All of these benefits may be achieved independently of the exact designation of the role as a Chief Artificial Intelligence Officer or not.

Moving from HR to HAIR

Beyond the question of establishing a Chief Artificial Intelligence Officer or not, the growing importance of AI affects multiple other business functions, especially HR. In many companies, HR is not the first department that actively addresses the opportunities and challenges of AI. In many other companies, however, HR is very advanced at least with regard to exploring the opportunities of AI. This may be somewhat surprising because, at first glance, HR experts may appear to be less well prepared to implement AI solutions than experts in other functions, such as IT or R&D. Nonetheless, many HR professionals have become aware of the opportunities of AI for their tasks at a relatively early moment, and they now actively implement selected AI solutions. While this openness is laudable and many AI activities that are related to HR have some clear benefits, the activities of most companies only focus on a subset of the implications of AI on the HR department so far.

To fully capture the benefits of AI for a company's HR in general and the HR department in particular, the scope and role of the HR department may well have to be extended. In fact, there may be major opportunities for a company's HR professionals in transforming the HR department into the HAIR department. This extended role of HAIR would refer to Human and Artificial Intelligence Resources.[4] Extending the scope and direction of the HR department towards AI may constitute a major challenge because the competencies that are required to fulfill this role will typically exceed the competencies that most HR functions presently have. Nonetheless, HR professionals should openly embrace this transformation and extension of their tasks and responsibilities because it is a major opportunity to further strengthen the impact of HR throughout the organization. Moreover, such a transformation makes perfect sense from an intelligence-based perspective because it facilitates an integrated intelligence architecture, involving human experts and virtual employees in terms of AI.

The focus of most HR departments with regard to AI has usually been limited to using AI for enhancing the completion of their traditional HR tasks. However, this is only one of the following three major dimensions that describe the impact of AI on HR. First, AI solutions may be applied by HR professionals. Second, beyond using AI for HR, executives need to consider the alternative perspective of supervising virtual employees.[5] This would refer to an equivalent of HR tasks for these virtual employees. Hence, we might refer to AIR activities, which stands for Artificial Intelligence Resources. Third, the HAIR responsibilities may specifically address the interdependencies of AI and HI in terms of the collaboration of human and virtual employees. This dimension includes optimizing the human-machine interfaces, but it goes beyond the mere interface management. For instance, the collaboration of humans and machines may also require redesigning established performance metrics to incorporate the growing importance of AI and the changing role of human experts that is associated with this transformation.

These three dimensions of the various implications at the intersection of AI and HR may be similarly essential in the long run, but the first dimension is most important in the near future.[6] HR departments may leverage AI solutions for enhancing their HR-related activities. Accordingly, HR professionals need to develop their own expertise or need to hire new colleagues to leverage the opportunities of AI in all parts of the HR management process. For instance, companies may rely on AI-based solutions for selecting the most promising employees. Here, the German company Precire Technologies has developed a solution that enables HR professionals to get an analysis of multiple character traits of a job candidate merely based on a relatively short telephone interview. As such, companies may replace expensive assessment centers, and the strongly growing quality of this AI solution enables recruiters to focus their own activities on their core tasks to further enhance their work outcomes. As such, companies may simultaneously strengthen the effectiveness and the efficiency of recruiting processes. In a similar vein, companies may rely on AI solutions to capture some of the tacit knowledge of key experts when they retire or move on to another job outside the firm. While it is usually not possible to capture all structured and unstructured insights and expertise, AI solutions provide new opportunities to retain and leverage some of this knowledge and intelligence.

Beyond the mere focus on leveraging AI in HR, a transformation towards HAIR responsibilities provides major opportunities for enabling Intelligence^X – comprising different types of AI, HI, and the meta-intelligence. Traditionally, HR does not have relevant competencies in people analytics or other fields of AI. In a similar vein, IT does not focus on many AI fields, especially with regard to product-related AI solutions. Even if companies have dedicated experts for people analytics and product-related AI solutions, this is typically insufficient for leveraging the interplay of AI, HI, and meta-intelligence. Exactly at this intersection, a HAIR department may provide a critical contribution with regard to succeeding in an intelligence-based business arena in the future. An alternative to the HAIR approach might be a cross-functional approach, which attempts to achieve integrated intelligence across multiple business functions – similar to a cross-functional innovation process, which has been established in many companies. Independently of the particular organizational approach, however, an extension of the HR department's tasks and responsibilities is beneficial in most cases. Thus, HR professionals should be open to transforming their own function towards integrating at least some aspects of HAIR management.

Chapter 14

The I3 – Integrated Intelligence Incubator

What are the implications of an intelligence-based perspective on company performance, and what measures can executives undertake in order to prepare their companies for an intelligence-based future? It is relatively easy to acknowledge the strategic relevance of AI. Actually taking the first steps towards implementing systematic AI activities is a different story, let alone the development of an integrated intelligence architecture. By now, the majority of companies does not have an awareness problem with regard to AI. The managerial challenges have rather shifted from generally exploring the phenomenon towards exploiting the opportunities while simultaneously avoiding the threats of AI for a company's competitive position. Accordingly, the core challenge is not a limited willingness or lacking strategic intent. The main difficulty further is not a specific detail of the operational implementation. Instead, a key problem for many organizations at present is the targeted implementation of AI initiatives with particular emphasis on linking the strategic plans with the initial stages of execution.

Many companies have experimented with selected AI applications. In some cases, these isolated activities have proved successful. In many other cases, the experiments have provided interesting insights, but the companies have not continued to fully implement these specific AI solutions. Often, executives are at a key decision point of taking bold steps towards using AI beyond this initial experimentation phase and beyond the selected use of some tools, such as customer service bots. However, this transition phase is often challenging, and many top executives see the challenge of moving into new fields without a clear understanding of whether the selected AI applications are a good choice or whether there might be more beneficial solutions that have not been considered yet. Of course, it is hardly possible to achieve a comprehensive overview of all potential AI opportunities and then to select only the very best options. What is feasible, however, is a systematic guideline that helps executives to find AI opportunities and potential blank spots of their extant AI activities in a structured way. At the very least, this systematic procedure allows for getting relatively close to the optimal managerial response to a disruptive evolution like AI.

In particular, a systematic guideline in the initial implementation stages helps executives to move beyond the experimentation stage for AI solutions. Moreover, it includes a company-level perspective to identify potential positive and negative synergies among the AI activities in different business units or functional units of large companies. Thus, it allows an appraisal of the digital innovation portfolio and selecting the right AI projects. This systematic company-wide implementation is beneficial for companies that just start with AI initiatives. However, it is also helpful for rebooting and optimizing ongoing AI initiatives. Many companies have already started such initiatives, but many of these initiatives have not taken off as initially planned. Some of the challenges may derive from an insufficient portfolio perspective as well as unclear responsibilities and competencies. An example is the role of the HR department and a potential transformation towards HAIR. Independent of the specific organizational solution, however, it is helpful to follow a clear step-by-step procedure that has proved suitable in many companies from a variety of sectors. This guideline is termed the I3 – Integrated Intelligence Incubator.

I3 – Integrated Intelligence Incubator

The term I3 – Integrated Intelligence Incubator indicates that it is a tool for supporting companies in advancing towards an integrated intelligence architecture. In particular, it allows firms to link their AI initiatives with their established business activities on the one hand and to explore new strategic opportunities and revenue streams on the other. Thus, it provides executives with a clear guideline for moving from strategic priority to operational action. While AI already enjoys a high strategic priority in many companies, the steps towards systematically implementing AI beyond selected experimental cases often is a major barrier. The stepwise procedure of the I3 – Integrated Intelligence Incubator further enables firms to go beyond an exclusive focus on AI and to systematically leverage the interdependencies of AI, HI, and the meta-intelligence. As such, it is a helpful tool for reacting to changes in a company's competitive environment due to AI and for proactively influencing a company's environment to deliberately shape the intelligence-based business. Following the guideline enables executives to set the conditions for achieving an intelligence-based competitive advantage.

Many companies respond to the recent advances in AI with isolated ignorance, as indicated in the upper part of Figure 11. If these companies pursue AI projects at all, these standalone projects are largely unconnected. Consequently, they do not realize the potential of AI for their business. In contrast, the I3 – Integrated Intelligence Incubator assumes a company-level perspective on the entire portfolio of AI activities, as indicated in the lower part of Figure 11. As such, it helps companies to respond to the recent advances in AI by selecting the most promising projects in an initial funnel. Furthermore, it supports executives in identifying blank spots that have not been addressed at all. Accordingly, the I3 –Integrated Intelligence Incubator enables businesses to achieve a competitive advantage by focusing on a portfolio of integrated projects that are implemented according to the regular project organization of the companies. To ease the step-by-step implementation of this procedure, two canvases are presented below, which support managers in following the ten steps of the I3 – Integrated Intelligence Incubator.

Specifically, the I3 – Integrated Intelligence Incubator comprises ten steps that lead executives from identifying major trends of AI for their particular business to managing the implementation of one or multiple projects based on a firm's individual project organization. Jointly, the projects add up to a firm's strategic AI initiative, which goes beyond mere AI is-

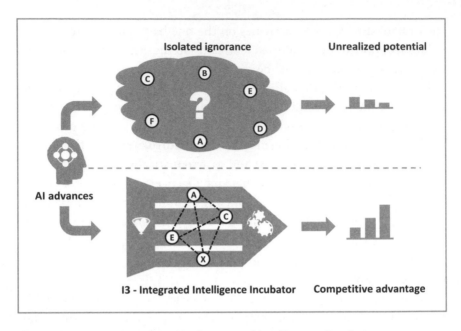

Figure 11: Illustration of the I3 – Integrated Intelligence Incubator

sues to provide the basis for developing an integrated intelligence architecture in the long run. The ten steps can be divided into two parts. The first part comprises steps 1–5, which assume a company-level perspective on the entire portfolio of AI activities and beyond. The core points of these steps may be displayed in the company canvas, which is illustrated in Figure 14. The second part comprises the subsequent steps 6–10. In contrast to the first part, it focuses on individual topics that may be implemented according to a company's regular project organization. Thus, it does not consider the entire project portfolio related to AI. Instead, it focuses on a single topic, and the core points of these steps may be displayed in the project canvas, which is illustrated in Figure 15. As such, a company needs to run through steps 1 to 5 once for the entire organization. Then, each project that is started based on the results of steps 1–5 needs to address steps 6–10 separately. On this basis, the I3 – Integrated Intelligence Incubator helps to keep an overview of the different projects in the digital innovation portfolio.

Company canvas

Step 1 – Major trends: At the beginning, organizations need to specify the major trends that affect their activities with regard to AI. Usually, executives already have some understanding of the relevance and potential consequences of AI. Otherwise, they would not usually have started an AI initiative in the first place. In many cases, however, companies are somewhat overwhelmed by the complexity and diversity of AI topics. Therefore, it is critical to clearly articulate and list the relevant influences of AI. This may refer to the different types of AI. For example, what machine learning technologies are likely to play an important role, and how might natural language processing affect a company's business activities? In addition, companies may consider different fields of applying AI in order to identify relevant trends. For instance, what role may AI play in different sectors that are related to a company's business activities?

Companies may undertake these analyses for AI and integrated intelligence as an overall topic. They may further extend the scope to consider all consequences of digital transformation beyond AI. In this regard, they may take into account the potential of data-based business opportunities in general without specifically focusing on AI. By contrast, companies may also focus more specifically on examining the relevant trends for a potential business unit only. In a similar vein, they may only concentrate on one type of AI to explore this particular field, such as speech synthesis, in more detail. In any way, the core output of this initial step is a systematic understanding of the most critical trends whose consequences will be analyzed more thoroughly in the following steps. Usually, it is helpful to list these trends in concise terms in the upper left corner of the company canvas. Accordingly, this first step helps executives to focus on those trends in the context of the general advances of AI that are most relevant for a company's future business.

Step 2 – Value chain: Based on the analysis of major trends, companies need to examine the impact of these trends on the value chain activities in their industry. AI has a specific impact in each sector and an even more individual impact on each company. However, there are two dimensions that are affected in nearly all industries, and the first of these dimensions is the value chain, which constitutes the horizontal dimension in the company canvas. In this regard, the value chain activities are often transformed and extended. Transformation here refers to changing and moving activities to a different stage in the value chain. Extension describes the emergence of new relevant value chain activities. In addition, some existing value chain activities may be largely unaffected by the changes and a company's competencies in these fields continue to be utilized as before (Figure 12). For example, AI and data analytics often encourage platform-based business models, which fulfill an integration function and which occupy the value chain position between a manufacturing firm and its traditional customers. Consequently, a manufacturing company my face the threat of losing its direct customer relationships and being downgraded to a mere hardware supplier for a service-based company like the platform provider.

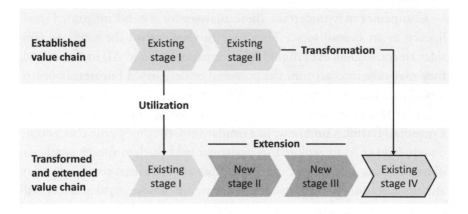

Figure 12: Extension of value chain

For example, a simplified established value chain in the automotive industry may comprise the following six basic activities: R&D, purchasing, production, marketing & sales, financial services, and aftersales services. In light of AI and related developments, which enable autonomous driving, two new activities become essential: mobility services and data analytics. In addition, two existing activities are moved to different stages of the value chain: aftersales services and financial services. On this basis, the value chain activities are extended and reorganized in the context of digitalization, AI, and other evolutions. Here, it is particularly critical to gain insights into the interplay of multiple trends and how they will jointly – rather than individually – affect the value chain activities in a company's industry. The core output of this step is a clear understanding of the future value chain in a company's industry. Usually, it is helpful to consider a company's own value chain steps as well as selected prior and subsequent stages. These renewed value chain stages in intelligence-based future competition are the basis for the horizontal dimension in the company canvas.

Step 3 – Value stakeholders: Drawing on the analysis of major trends in the first step, companies may also identify various stakeholders, which will be relevant for generating value in their business activities in an intelligence-based future. These value stakeholders are the second dimension that is affected by the growing role of AI in nearly all industries. As such, it constitutes the vertical dimension in the company canvas. Typically, this list of stakeholders includes some players that have been relevant in a company's industry for a long time. In particular, it tends to comprise the 'usual suspects', such as a company's suppliers, customers in different segments, and potential alliance partners. Beyond these established players, there may be additional new stakeholders in intelligence-based ecosystems, which only start playing a role due to the higher importance of AI and related evolutions. Here, it is often helpful to consider relevant technology enablers from a technology push perspective and major market applications from a market pull perspective (Figure 13).

For instance, established stakeholders from the perspective of an automotive company include suppliers, customers, competitors, dealers, investors, and regulators. In the context of AI, autonomous driving and related advances, some additional stakeholders become relevant. A technology push perspective on relevant trends may lead to further considering IT service providers, infrastructure providers, and technology giants like Google and Apple. A trend analysis based on market pull logic may further point to the importance of mobility providers, data-based service

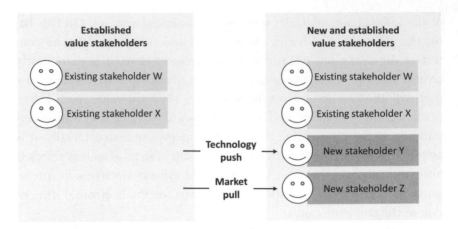

Figure 13: Extension of stakeholders

partners, and content providers. Similar to the value chain activities, the list of stakeholders in a company's environment is extended, and their role partly changes. For example, well-known competitors may increasingly become partners, whereas new competitors emerge from different sectors. The critical output of this step is a meaningful list of key stakeholders that will be relevant in a data-driven and intelligence-based business context in the future.

Step 4 – Core fields: Jointly, the extended value chain activities and the list of value stakeholders provide the basis for the company canvas, which is displayed in Figure 14.[1] Here, the different fields may be used to indicate which stakeholders are relevant for which value chain activities. Some of the fields will be a company's home turf. This is usually where a firm's traditional value chain activities meet the 'usual suspects', such as established customers, suppliers, and competitors. Beyond this home turf, there may be many areas that are less familiar to a company. Some of these areas may not have been important in the past, and they may also not become important in the foreseeable future. Hence, these fields do not deserve particular attention. However, executives need to proceed carefully to avoid quickly discarding some activities related to particular stakeholders although these fields may in fact become critical in the future. The key target of this step is to identify the core fields for intelligence-based competition in the future. These core fields may include some areas, which have been core fields for a company in the past. In addition, however, the growing role of AI typically leads to an increasing relevance of some new fields.

In the automotive industry, for example, the intersection of the new value chain activity 'data analytics' with the new stakeholder 'mobility provider' may enable completely new business models. These business models strongly draw on AI solutions, but their impact goes far beyond mere AI. As such, these business models will strongly affect the established activities of automotive companies. Therefore, this is certainly a core field for automotive companies. Hence, the essential output of this step is to further condense and channel the insights from the analyses of trends, value chain activities, and value stakeholders in the previous steps based on a systematic framework. This overview provides a sound basis for further discussions, and it may enable organizational learning beyond the individual learning of employees in different parts of the organization. On this basis, executives may identify those fields that are particularly promising or risky in the context of AI in order to direct their attention to these core fields in the subsequent steps.

Step 5 – Key points: After identifying the core fields in the previous step, companies need to analyze the key points in each field. Here, the key points refer to the gain points and/or pain points of the relevant stakeholder in the particular value chain activity. In this step, firms may rely on a variety of creativity techniques and especially design thinking approaches. Usually, it is relatively easy to articulate some gain points, which would provide a clear benefit to the stakeholder, or pain points, which the stakeholder would want to avoid.[2] Executives may bring together some internal experts from different functional units across the organization in a workshop setting and make them familiar with the company canvas in Figure 14. Typically, this cross-functional group may provide at least some convincing starting points for identifying the key points for each field. In the automotive industry, for example, the core field of data analytics with regard to customers may lead to discussions about the key points of a driver's daily commute to work. This discussion would emphasize the need for advanced algorithms to anticipate as exactly as possible what value-added services could match with the gain points and pain points of an individual driver.

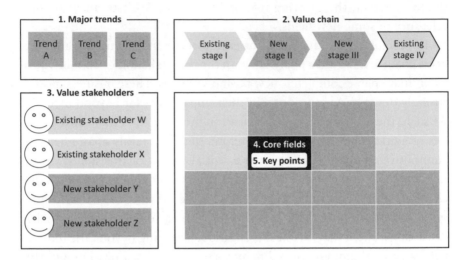

Figure 14: Company canvas

Based on an initial identification of key points, companies may rely on additional design thinking methods, such as observing and interviewing stakeholders to specify the particular gain points and pain points. These key points do not yet include an idea or concept for a potential solution. Rather, this step focuses on identifying potential advantages and drawbacks for the stakeholders in the core fields in a future intelligence-based context. Independently of the particular solution, the gain points and pain points may be identified from a market pull or technology push perspective. The market pull perspective starts with the needs and wishes of the stakeholder and puts them in the perspective of an intelligence-based future setting. In contrast, the technology push perspective starts with the impact of AI on the particular activities of the stakeholder in this value chain step and examines potential gain points and pain points on that basis. Then, the key points can be prioritized. In addition, it is often possible to group some of the most relevant points, for example by linking them according to a particular stakeholder or value chain step or by integrating them with regard to their content. For example, multiple gain points and pain points may require the collection and smart analysis of large volumes of related data. Ideally, the output of this step is a manageable number of strategic topics, which each comprise a group of related gain points and pain points.

By finishing step 5, companies successfully complete the first part of the I3 – Integrated Intelligence Incubator. In this first part, a relatively broad perspective is assumed by examining the project portfolio related to AI at the level of the entire company or business unit. The outcome of these initial steps 1–5 is a systematic overview of the future intelligence-based business context along with some prioritized strategic topics that deserve further attention in the next steps. The value of this systematic framework at the portfolio level should not be underestimated. It can also be used to map some of a company's ongoing AI initiatives to understand their particular strategic focus. Usually, this analysis will also lead to identifying some blank spots that have not been addressed so far. In addition, it may contribute to identifying positive and negative synergies among multiple AI initiatives that are often separately conducted in different parts of a large organization. As such, this first part of the I3 – Integrated Intelligence Incubator strongly contributes to achieving an integrated intelligence architecture.

Project canvas

For each of the strategic topics that are identified in the first part of the I3 – Integrated Intelligence Incubator, a company addresses steps 6–10 separately. Here, the focus is on developing concepts in the initial stages of a single project for each strategic topic. If organizations already have some ongoing AI activities, which are often managed in relative isolation, the first part typically leads to focusing on the most promising projects. Accordingly, the number of topics is reduced based on the initial funnel. This is illustrated in Figure 11, where only projects A, C, and E are pursued in the lower part in contrast to projects A-F in the upper part of the figure. Moreover, the first part of the I3 – Integrated Intelligence Incubator typically leads to the identification of further promising fields, which had been overlooked before. This is indicated in Figure 11 by pursuing project X in the lower part, which does not exist in the upper part of the figure. To develop detailed concepts for the most promising topics, firms may rely on the project canvas that is presented in Figure 15 and that should be addressed for each prioritized strategic topic. If this project canvas is completed, executives will have all the necessary information to approve the concept and to start a formal implementation project with a separate budget based on a firm's regular project organization.

Step 6 – Value proposition: To advance from the strategic topics towards clear managerial actions, it is helpful to rely on the business model logic, which enables companies to arrive at a prioritized number of projects with a business plan. This list of projects that are ready for implementation will be the outcome of the second part of the I3 – Integrated Intelligence Incubator, and the business model logic is essential in this second part. Without discussing more detailed business model segmentations, such as the business model canvas[3], a business model generally comprises three major components: value proposition, value generation, and value capture. The value proposition is the key link between the strategic topics that have been identified in step 5 and the further activities in step 6–10. For each strategic topic, a company tries to develop a convincing value proposition in response to the gain points and pain points that have been specified in step 5. Usually, the strategic topics will comprise several of these points, and the value proposition addresses these points.

In this regard, a company may rely on additional desk research and design thinking methods like customer interviews in order to shape the potential value proposition. Here, it is useful to note that the value propositions do not exclusively address a company's customers. Rather, they may be directed at all of the stakeholders that are listed in the company canvas in Figure 14. In the context of AI, companies increasingly need to think in terms of ecosystems to offer suitable solutions to their customers. To be able to offer these definitive solutions, it may be essential to have clear value propositions for ecosystem partners and other stakeholders. Thus, the value proposition articulates the value that is offered to the particular value stakeholders. The core output of this step is a clear value proposition, and it should be displayed at the heart of the project canvas, which is illustrated in Figure 15. Often, it is helpful to write down a short and catchy statement of the value proposition along with a more detailed description, which captures all relevant content that has been generated so far. In addition, it is useful to explain how the value proposition may contribute to a potential competitive advantage.

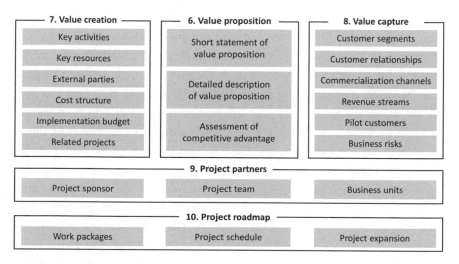

Figure 15: Project canvas

Step 7 – Value creation: Based on a convincing value proposition, firms need to further detail their value creation activities for the specific strategic topic. In particular, this step requires a firm's experts to shape the solution that they plan to offer to the value stakeholders in more detail. As such, business model experts need to orchestrate the ecosystem and the value chain activities to provide the particular value proposition for the stakeholders' needs. Following the logic of the business model canvas[4], a company needs to consider the key activities that need to be accomplished for offering the value proposition. Moreover, executives need an overview of the key resources and potential external partners in the ecosystem and other external parties in the broader environment. Some of the external partners may already be listed in the company canvas, but some of them may only be relevant in a particular value creation activity for this strategic topic.

On this basis, the mapping of the value creation content needs to include a detailed understanding of the relevant cost structure and implementation budget, which are associated with the value proposition. Furthermore, this step is key for examining the interdependencies of the value creation activities with a company's other activities and with related projects in order to identify potential synergies and interfaces. It is important to clarify the interactions of new AI solutions with a company's existing AI and HI. The integration of the AI solutions with a company's existing intelligence architecture is a key issue for achieving a potential competitive advantage, and it deserves sufficient attention in this step. The core output of this step is a thorough understanding of the value creation activities, and the major points should be added to the left part of the project canvas in Figure 15. Here, executives need to pay particular attention to a high level of alignment between value creation and the value proposition in the center of the project canvas.

Step 8 – Value capture: Based on the analyses of value proposition and value creation in the previous steps, companies need to address the value capture part of the business model, which is critical for ensuring that a company will actually profit from its plans concerning AI and new digital solutions. Here, a company's experts may again draw on the logic of the business model canvas[5] in order to examine relevant customer segments, customer relationships, and commercialization channels in a systematic way. In particular, this discussion highlights the impact of the value proposition beyond a firm's existing business activities. So far, many AI initiatives have focused on optimizing a company's internal processes by capturing efficiency benefits. Consequently, the core of this value appropriation refers to optimization and cost reduction in traditional business activities. Alternatively, firms may rely on AI to develop innovative solutions that result in completely new revenue streams that extend a company's previous business activities. In established companies, many AI solutions will lead to intelligent services rather than to hardware products or to the commercialization of data.

These intelligent services may be offered for free in order to strengthen the sales of a company's physical products. Alternatively, the intelligent services may become an independent product or complementary product to a company's existing products. These different possibilities underscore the need for a clear understanding of the value capture part of the business model. As such, this step also involves the completion of a business plan, including a forecast of the expected revenue streams as well as potential business risks and pilot customers. The central output of this step is a detailed overview of the value capture activities, and the major points should be displayed in the right part of the project canvas in Figure 15. On this basis, a comparison of the value creation and value capture part, including the cost structure and revenue streams, allows for analyzing the expected financial impact of realizing a value proposition. Here, it is important to consider the potentially exponential growth of data-based and intelligence-based business models as well as the role of intelligent services for the future sales of a company's current products. In many situations, AI components and intelligent services will be required for enjoying strong product sales in the future. Thus, many companies do not really have another option than moving into AI and related fields.

Step 9 – Project partners: Besides identifying the core components of the business model, it is essential to get a thorough overview of the relevant project partners. Here, it is important to identify a suitable project sponsor. Ideally, this person is part of a company's top management team and fully committed to the project. Rather than operationally participating in the project, the sponsor promotes and champions the project based on a strong personal network, budget, and hierarchical power. A suitable project sponsor may play a decisive role in achieving the top executives' commitment and formal approval for implementation. Beyond the project sponsor, the members of the core project team need to be defined. Usually, it is helpful keep the number of core team members relatively low in order to ensure flexibility and agile processes. In addition, several persons may be part of an extended project team, and they will be strongly involved on an ad-hoc basis when their contribution is actually needed. Thus, the time and resources of these persons are only accessed when necessary.

This approach to staffing the project team follows the 'lean startup' logic, which reduces the necessary investment in the early stages and which is used in many AI projects.[6] Besides potentially lowering the initial implementation budget, it often helps to speed up internal project management. Beyond the project team, it is usually important to closely involve one or multiple business units whose activities are related to the project. In many cases, AI projects have a particularly strong impact on a specific business unit. Even if the project has a broad impact – or if it may lead to a completely new business unit after implementation – it is helpful to initially focus on some pilot applications in one business unit. Therefore, it is helpful to clarify the potential interdependencies with a firm's remaining business activities at the beginning. Often, it may be possible to merge some of the activities and budgets of corporate-level and business unit-level AI activities, leading to cross-pollination and synergies. The output of this step is a list of critical project partners, including the project sponsor, core team members, extended team members as well as relevant business units, which need to be involved along the project roadmap. These stakeholders should be integrated in the lower part of the project canvas in Figure 15.

Step 10 – Project roadmap: Beyond a detailed analysis of the business model, the project canvas includes a thorough plan for the next steps. As such, a firm's experts should list the work packages that need to be completed to bring a new business model to the market in as much detail as possible. This implementation focus is particularly important because the I3 – Integrated Intelligence Incubator only covers the fuzzy front end activities of implementing AI solutions. As such, it comprises the key activities from the analyses of relevant trends and generating initial ideas to developing concepts, business models, and business cases until the decision is taken to actually start further development and execution. A proficient management of this fuzzy front end is critical because many promising AI initiatives fail in a relatively early phase. Once a company's executives have approved the start of a formal development project, many companies have systematic development and project management tools in place to ensure that the project successfully approaches market launch or internal implementation. By contrast, this systematic management is often lacking in the early stages of ideation, concept development, and business model design until the executive decision is taken to initiate a formal project.

Therefore, the I3 – Integrated Intelligence Incubator is particularly important in light of the complexity of many AI solutions and their linkages to the other parts of an organization's intelligence architecture. Accordingly, a detailed project schedule is needed in this step.

In addition, the project roadmap allows for displaying the next levels of a value proposition and strategic topic. Although this aspect goes beyond the particular project, it is critical because of the rapid technological evolution in many fields of AI and the complexity of many intelligence-based solutions and data-based business models. Therefore, companies often start with developing a first level of a particular solution, service, or component. This first-level solution already involves some AI functionalities, but it typically does not comprise all potential functionalities that may be feasible in a few years. Therefore, the execution project initially focuses on implementing the first level of the solution, and the section about project expansion helps to document the additional ideas and concepts that a company's experts have along the course of the project for further improving an initial minimum viable product. Beyond this approach, however, AI solutions often need to be customized to a company's particular requirements. Therefore, it is usually beneficial to start with some quick-win functionalities and later expand upon the initial version based on the specific conditions and use cases of a company. Thus, companies may already plan the expansion and renewal of their value proposition in the context of further technological advances and new market trends for the relevant value stakeholders. The output of this step is a detailed list of work packages, project schedules, and project expansions. This list of key activities, deadlines, and functionalities for the future is shown at the bottom of the project canvas in Figure 15. On this basis, a company's executives have all the relevant information for immediately taking the decision to implement the project based on the required budget.

Implementation checklist

By completing the ten steps of the I3 – Integrated Intelligence Incubator, companies may systematically link the general analysis of trends related to AI with the implementation of their regular development projects for

Canvas	Steps	Checklist items	Results
Company canvas	1. Major trends	■ Which major trends affect our established business activities? ■ Which major trends provide completely new business opportunities in the future? ■ How will the digital transformation of the industry impact our future business? ■ How will advances in different fields of AI affect our future business?	Prioritized strategic topics
	2. Value chain	■ Which existing value chain activities are continued in the future? ■ Which existing value chain activities become less relevant? ■ Which existing value chain activities are transformed? ■ Which new activities extend the established value chain?	
	3. Value stakeholders	■ Which existing stakeholders continue to be important? ■ Which existing stakeholders become less relevant? ■ Which new stakeholders emerge from a technology push or market pull perspective? ■ How will the ecosystem of value stakeholders change in the future?	

Canvas	Steps	Checklist items	Results
Company canvas	4. Core fields	■ Which value chain activities are particularly relevant for which stakeholders? ■ Which new combinations of value chain activities and stakeholders are particularly important? ■ Which of the fields that are our 'home turf' deserve particular attention in the future? ■ Where are potential white spaces of ongoing digital transformation and AI initiatives?	Prioritized strategic topics
	5. Key points	■ What are the key strategic issues for our future business in each of the core fields? ■ What are major gain points or pain points of the relevant stakeholders in each core field? ■ How can the different key points be prioritized based on additional information? ■ How can the prioritized key points be grouped into strategic topics based on their content?	
Project canvas	6. Value proposition	■ What is the value that we can offer the stakeholders for each prioritized strategic topic? ■ How does the value proposition address the stakeholders' gain points or pain points? ■ How can the value proposition be described in a short statement and in more detail? ■ How does the value proposition contribute to achieving a competitive advantage?	Aligned implementation projects

Canvas	Steps	Checklist items	Results
Project canvas	7. Value creation	■ What are the key activities and key resources for addressing the value proposition? ■ Which external ecosystem partners need to be orchestrated to develop a solution? ■ What is the cost structure, and which synergies with other related projects are relevant? ■ What implications does this value creation have for the integrated intelligence architecture?	Aligned implementation projects
	8. Value capture	■ How can we profit from the AI solution beyond strengthening internal efficiency? ■ What are relevant customer segments and customer relationships for the new solution? ■ Which types of revenue streams may be generated in which commercialization channels? ■ How does the business plan capture potential risks and exponential growth of the solution?	
	9. Project partners	■ Who is the project sponsor, who is part of the core team and of the extended project team? ■ How can we get the top executives' commitment and formal approval for implementation? ■ Which business units need to be closely involved in the course of the project? ■ How can the lean startup approach help to speed up internal project organization?	

Canvas	Steps	Checklist items	Results
Project canvas	10. Project roadmap	■ Which work packages need to be completed to market the new business model? ■ What is the project schedule and necessary budget for implementation? ■ Which improvements and expansions of the first solution may be considered later? ■ Which new functionalities may be technologically feasible in the foreseeable future?	Aligned implementation projects

Table 5: Checklist for the ten steps of the I3 –
Integrated Intelligence Incubator

new solutions. Starting from the major trends related to AI and digitalization, executives may systematically move along steps 1 to 5 of the I3 – Integrated Intelligence Incubator once for the entire organization. Here, the company canvas helps map the insights of steps 1 to 5. The checklist items in Table 5 offer further guiding questions for thoroughly covering the critical content of these steps. As an outcome, firms have convincingly identified prioritized strategic topics. Subsequently, each prioritized topic needs to proceed along steps 6–10 separately. Here, the project canvas provides a useful framework. To further ease the implementation of these steps, the checklist items offer helpful starting points. As an outcome of these steps, companies have a number of aligned projects that are ready for implementation according to their typical project organization.

On this basis, the I3 – Integrated Intelligence Incubator has proved helpful for moving from acknowledging the strategic relevance of AI to executing suitable development and implementation projects. In particular, the I3 – Integrated Intelligence Incubator is a helpful tool for visualizing the context of specific AI initiatives for a company's top executives.

In addition, it helps to contextualize envisioned projects, to align multiple projects in a portfolio, and to provide convincing arguments why specific budgets for developing, utilizing, and commercializing AI solutions are beneficial from a strategic point of view. Furthermore, this approach is helpful for identifying blank spots in a company's ongoing AI initiatives and for aligning and leveraging the synergies among multiple AI initiatives that have often been started in relative isolation in different parts of large firms. Thus, the I3 – Integrated Intelligence Incubator contributes to enhancing the financial impact of AI activities by optimizing their strategic direction and design in the early implementation stages. As such, it is a helpful tool for companies that are just starting an AI initiative as well as for companies that already have several ongoing AI activities.

Moreover, the I3 – Integrated Intelligence Incubator enables companies to align their AI initiatives with their established product business and organizational processes. Thus, it allows for systematically identifying core interfaces between new AI solutions and a company's other HI and AI. These interdependencies are important when AI is used for enhancing the efficiency of ongoing business processes. They are even more important, however, when AI is used for innovation in terms of developing new solutions. In most cases, the new solutions will not be completely independent from a firm's established business activities. Rather, they will intelligently extend and complement a company's activities, and a systematic mapping of the interrelationships between a company's traditional business and its future intelligence-based business is a unique strength of the I3 – Integrated Intelligence Incubator, which has proved successful in many projects with companies from diverse sectors. As such, it is a key tool for generating organizational learning and advancing from isolated ignorance towards integrated intelligence (Table 6).

In particular, an integrated intelligence architecture enables companies to move from strategic awareness to operational action with regard to AI. Moreover, it contributes to establishing convincing company-level initiatives beyond isolated ad-hoc activities for implementing specific AI solutions. In this regard, isolated ignorance and integrated intelligence constitute the extreme points of a continuum, and most companies are located between these two extremes. On this basis, the I3 – Integrated In-

Criteria	Isolated ignorance	Integrated intelligence
Approach	■ Ad-hoc application of individual AI solutions ■ Stand-alone use of AI to replace human work ■ Ignorance or activism with limited direction ■ Individual project perspective	■ Company-level coordination of strategic AI initiatives ■ Complementarity with human expertise ■ Synergies and alignment with business strategy ■ Project and portfolio perspective
Learning	■ Focus on AI and separate human intelligence ■ Primary emphasis on individual learning	■ Intelligence^x with AI, human intelligence, and meta-intelligence ■ Individual as well as organizational learning
Advantage	■ Limited scope of AI activities with blank spots ■ Efficiency focus ■ Strong emphasis on technology domain	■ Broader scope of AI activities to leverage the entire strategy space ■ Balancing efficiency and innovation ■ Strategic emphasis on business model
Impact	■ Enhancing established processes and maintaining a traditional competitive advantage ■ Unrealized opportunities and neglected potential	■ Gaining and sustaining an intelligence-based competitive advantage over time ■ Interface management for integrated intelligence architecture

Table 6: Isolated ignorance vs. integrated intelligence

telligence Incubator enables companies to achieve Intelligence^x – encompassing various types of AI and HI as well as the meta-intelligence. While the I3 – Integrated Intelligence Incubator may be completed in a relatively short period, the development of an integrated intelligence architecture usually is a gradual and complex process rather than a quick switch from one day to another. In this regard, it may well be compared with transforming an organizational culture over time. Even if such a major change requires considerable time and effort, it is essential to take the first steps, because most companies will not have another option than embracing intelligence-based competition in the long run, and the I3 – Integrated Intelligence Incubator is a good starting point for this journey.

Chapter 15

Avoiding typical pitfalls in execution

Many companies have started successful AI initiatives, though not all of them have been successful so far. Furthermore, most of the companies that have successfully implemented some AI applications openly admit that they are still at the very beginning of leveraging the opportunities that are associated with AI. Moreover, even the most advanced companies concede that they are relatively far away from an integrated intelligence architecture, which would require a systematic management of the interplay of HI and AI as well as a continuous renewal and recombination of the different types of intelligence. Thus, even the most advanced companies may benefit from applying the I3 – Integrated Intelligence Incubator because it will help them to systematically identify at least some blank spots, which have not yet received sufficient attention. Combining the insights from the companies that have achieved some success in the context of AI with the lessons that had to be learned by less successful ones leads to an overview of typical pitfalls in executing AI initiatives.

Beyond gaining an understanding of typical pitfalls, the insights from the AI initiatives of other companies provide a general strategic direction for avoiding these pitfalls or at least for reducing their negative consequences. In this regard, some methods and tools may be particularly helpful. An overview of typical pitfalls, avoidance strategies, and helpful tools is given in Table 7. The ten typical pitfalls do not constitute a comprehensive list of managerial challenges and problems. However, they do represent typical problems that may be observed in many companies from different sectors.[1] These pitfalls can be further categorized according to their main emphasis on the technology, market, or management domain. This categorization does not imply that one of the pitfalls does not affect the other domains, but there is often a focus on the particular domain. Moreover, the methods and tools only present a selection rather than a full overview. In particular, there are tools like the I3 – Integrated Intelligence Incubator to help companies to avoid several of the pitfalls.

Domain	Typical pitfall	Avoidance strategies	Selected methods and tools
Technology	1. Over-emphasis on technology	Consider the market and value chain implications!	■ Value chain analysis ■ Forecasting market trends ■ Jobs to be done perspective
	2. Isolated stand-alone projects	Manage the portfolio of AI and digital projects systematically!	■ Project portfolio management ■ Strategic fit analysis ■ Firm-level collaboration
	3. Mere substitution of human intelligence	Benefit from the interdependencies of human and artificial intelligence!	■ Complementarity analysis ■ Studying inter-dependencies ■ Synthesis perspective
Market	4. Limited attention to customer needs	Thoroughly evaluate customer expectations!	■ Gain points and pain points ■ Design thinking personas ■ Use cases and user stories
	5. Over-emphasis on efficiency	Leverage the full potential for growth and innovation!	■ Company canvas ■ Innovation fields ■ Blue ocean perspective
	6. Lacking business model innovation	Deliberately challenge the dominant managerial logic!	■ Dominant logic analysis ■ Business ecosystem analysis ■ Business model canvas

Domain	Typical pitfall	Avoidance strategies	Selected methods and tools
Management	7. Limited artificial intelligence expertise	Accumulate knowhow in AI and digital transformation!	▪ HR development ▪ Hiring policy ▪ External consultants
	8. Aimless short-term activism	Develop a long-term vision for the digital future!	▪ Digital future story ▪ Empowering the Chief Digital Officer ▪ Investor relations
	9. Limited involvement of organization	Encourage the participation of employees at all levels!	▪ Participatory organization ▪ Change management ▪ Communities of practice
	10. Excessive level of perfectionism	Enable agile experimentation across the organization!	▪ Agile processes ▪ Failure tolerance ▪ Lean startup

Table 7: Overview of typical pitfalls (Source: partly adapted from Lichtenthaler, 2018, Ideen- und Innovationsmanagement[2])

Technology domain

Pitfall 1 – Overemphasis on technology: In managing their AI initiatives, many companies focus excessively on the technological challenges. Yes, new technologies are the basis for AI opportunities. However, the technological trends and the new technological solutions per se do not have a disruptive impact. Rather, the new AI solutions partly enable completely new offerings for a company's customers and other stakeholders. Consequently, the market and industry conditions may change substantially, and it is this change that leads to the disruption of industries and business models. These market-related consequences and challenges are often neglected or only analyzed superficially. To avoid this typical pitfall, executives need to consider the market and value chain implications of AI in detail. Besides forecasting market trends, it is essential to examine the impact of different AI solutions on the value chain in a company's industry. Here, it is often helpful to examine the 'jobs to be done'[3] in the value chain in order to identify particular tasks, which may be accomplished by different technologies and which may be affected by AI. These analyses should be done before a specific AI solution is selected, potentially along with the choice for a particular IT service provider. The alternative approach of first selecting a service provider and a specific IT solution and considering market expectations and business models only afterwards, is a typical source of implementation problems.

Pitfall 2 – Isolated stand-alone projects: Especially in large companies, multiple AI and digital transformation initiatives were started in the past years. This is helpful because many companies will be unable to respond to the growing importance of AI with a single measure only. In addition, it is often beneficial to pursue some AI activities at the level of individual business units and some other activities at corporate level. However, this generally positive strategic intent has often led to a situation in which multiple technology development projects are conducted in a relatively isolated way. Assigning a Chief Artificial Intelligence Officer or a Chief Digital Officer may help, but a dedicated role alone usually does not ensure a proficient orchestration of the diverse AI and digital innovation projects. Rather, companies need a systematic portfolio management of their AI projects. A targeted direction and ongoing management of these projects is essential because of mutual interdependencies. For example, an extended database with a new frontend at corporate level may rely on AI to enable personalized customer interactions of different business units to commercialize new services. Beyond a systematic portfolio management, executives need to put particular emphasis on strategic fit between the variety of AI activities and an organization's business and innovation strategies. In addition, an active collaboration and communication across multiple departments is needed to overcome the isolated management of diverse AI projects.

Pitfall 3 – Mere substitution of human intelligence: Another technology-related problem of many AI initiatives is their strong focus on replacing HI. This pitfall can often be traced back to viewing AI as a tool that can contribute to the optimization of established processes. Rather than imagining potential benefits from the interdependencies of AI and HI, many companies limit the scope of their AI initiatives to the mere substitution of human work. Of course, the efficiency gains that may be achieved from this substitution are important, and it is often easier to implement such AI solutions without changing the underlying processes and business models. However, this focus automatically neglects a large part of additional benefits, which could be identified by systematically analyzing pooled, sequential, or reciprocal interdependencies. In many situations, the complementarities of AI and HI point to a synthesis perspective, which enables various ideas and concepts for developing novel solutions that go beyond a company's current products, processes, and services. By combining AI with HI, companies may further implement solutions that are more difficult to imitate for competitors than the isolated application of AI solutions. In addition, the combination of AI solutions and human expertise contributes to overcoming the technology focus of merely considering AI solutions as stand-alone tools.

Market domain

Pitfall 4 – Limited attention to customer needs: A typical market-related pitfall of AI initiatives is lacking attention to the needs and expectations of a company's customers and further stakeholders. While this problem is related to an overemphasis on technology, it goes beyond a general technology focus. Specifically, many companies neglect to thoroughly evaluate the expectations that their customers have with regard to intelligent products, services, and solutions. Consequently, many companies spend substantial time and resources on developing solutions with a limited level of desirability from the perspective of customers or other relevant stakeholders. To avoid this pitfall, a company's experts may rely on design thinking approaches to understand the expectations of the other parties in more detail. This may include, for example, the development of personas and the analyses of their gain points and pain points as a basis for a value proposition that actually meets customer expectations. Focusing on specific use cases and developing convincing user stories further contributes to selecting those features for new products, services, and solutions that are actually required and desired by customers. For example, if many potential customers in a company's target segment are still reluctant to interact with AI based on underlying No-Human-Interaction attitudes, some new functionalities may actually be detrimental for a company's business even if they are promising from a technology and financial perspective.

Pitfall 5 – Overemphasis on efficiency: Another market-related pitfall is an excessive focus on enhancing efficiency, which is the primary strategic direction of many companies' AI initiatives. Of course, the cost benefits of using AI are important. However, this focus usually leads to neglecting the generation of growth and innovation in order to realize new revenue streams. So far, only a minority of companies leverage the potential of AI in this regard. In fact, the creative combination of AI solutions with a firm's human expertise and established products and services may enable new offerings with a major growth potential. There may be 'blue ocean' opportunities in terms of generating new markets with limited competition and with a high potential for sustained competitive advantage.[4] However, these 'blue oceans' partly require abstracting from a firm's current core business and from the 'red ocean' markets with intense competition. Consequently, these extended opportunities are often neglected because many companies have the tendency to stick to their core business and to use AI primarily for further optimizing this core business. In this regard, the company canvas of the I3 – Integrated Intelligence Incubator suggests some specific steps that help executives to tap into these 'blue oceans'. Companies may further combine this approach with an analysis of their major fields of innovation in order to select the most promising AI projects for innovation. Usually, these projects will extend a company's core business, while still leveraging some of the core competencies and resources in its established markets.

Pitfall 6 – Lacking business model innovation: By now, most executives have acknowledged the impact of AI and digital transformation more generally. However, the full impact of these disruptive changes on a company's core business is often underestimated. Most companies still expect that the majority of their business processes and their overall business model will continue to be relevant. This may be correct in most cases, but there may be a few changes that have dramatic consequences. Many companies are insufficiently prepared to these transformations because they are characterized by a dominant managerial logic, which involves some basic assumptions about the success factors of doing business in a particular industry, for example about product lifecycles, development budgets, and customers' willingness to pay. This dominant logic emerged when AI did not yet play a role in most firms. Moreover, many executives gained the top positions in their companies at a time when the relevance of AI was limited. Usually, AI will not challenge all success factors. However, there may be some critical transformation of the underlying business assumptions, and it requires rethinking a firm's dominant managerial logic and business model. Accordingly, executives need to thoroughly examine the changes in their industry and business ecosystem to shape their future business models. Following the components of the business model canvas may be helpful for discussing the business model implications of AI in a systematic way.

Management domain

Pitfall 7 – Limited AI expertise: Besides technology-related and market-related pitfalls of AI initiatives, there are often major challenges that derive specifically from the management of these initiatives. One of these challenges is the limited AI expertise in many established firms. This problem comprises a limited number of AI experts as well as a limited understanding of basic AI technologies among the top management team. There is no need for top executives to become experts in AI technology. However, it is important that a company's top management has some basic insights into the relevant technologies to thoroughly assess their market and strategic impact – or at least challenging a firm's internal experts in this regard. Although many established companies collaborate with specialized external service providers to implement particular AI solutions, it is usually important to have some internal experts for the most relevant fields of AI. As many companies are currently trying to hire such experts, firms often have difficulties filling their open positions. In the short run, it may therefore be helpful to collaborate with external consultants and freelancers. In the long run, however, there is often no alternative to hiring some full-time experts because they may also provide an important contribution in selecting the optimal AI solutions and external service providers. In addition, companies need to strengthen HR development activities in order to accumulate knowledge in AI and digital transformation at all hierarchical levels across the organization.

Pitfall 8 – Aimless short-term activism: Many companies have been relatively slow at acknowledging the strategic relevance of AI and subsequently implementing AI solutions. To compensate for this relatively late start, many firms hectically move forward with some AI activities. Often, however, these moves primarily represent short-term activism rather than well-designed strategic initiatives. In response to competitors' activities, companies may start collaborating with the same or similar service providers to implement some AI solutions. Of course, it is helpful to get going, and it is useful to experiment with several AI applications. However, these short-term activities need to be complemented by a long-term vision for the intelligence-based future. Otherwise, a company will have difficulties to manage the portfolio of its AI activities and to ensure strategic fit simply because there is no overall strategic direction. In this regard, executives need to put particular emphasis on developing a convincing storyline for the digital future. Based on a proficient communication of the AI activities, the market acceptance of new solutions can be eased, which facilitates further communication and which may finally lead to a self-reinforcing cycle of growing business activities based on AI. Beyond the market impact, a long-term vision is further critical for convincing investors and further stakeholders that a company will play an important future role.

Moreover, companies need to empower the Chief Digital Officer or any other person that oversees the AI activities because they often lack sufficient reach within the organization.

Pitfall 9 – Limited involvement of organization: Another typical pitfall in managing AI initiatives is a limited involvement of employees in various parts of the organization. In light of the relatively complex nature of AI, it is a natural course of action to set up a dedicated project with a few team members who focus on the implementation of AI. While this approach may help companies to establish isolated AI activities, it is usually insufficient for leveraging the potential of AI for the entire organization. In this regard, it is necessary to encourage the participation of employees at all levels across the organization. Otherwise, companies will be unable to advance towards an integrated intelligence architecture. The human expertise of employees from different organizational units may be needed in order to complement AI solutions. In addition, these people may have critical insights for enhancing the implementation of AI tools and for developing new products, services, and solutions at the intersection of AI and HI. Beyond a dedicated project team, companies may therefore rely on a participatory organizational approach and on change management initiatives for tapping into the ideas and suggestions of multiple organizational members. In addition, companies may establish informal communities of practice that focus on selected fields of AI to explore opportunities beyond the formal AI initiatives that have already been started.

Pitfall 10 – Excessive level of perfectionism: Finally, another typical pitfall is an excessive level of perfectionism in implementing AI initiatives. While this point may appear to contradict the fact that short-term activism is detrimental, this is true only at first glance. In fact, companies need to balance a long-term vision with enabling agile experimentation across the organization. When taking the initial steps of implementing AI solutions, many companies attempt to directly provide a perfect solution for the future. This expectation is commendable, but it needs to go along with sufficient pragmatism if an optimal solution is not possible in the first step. The term 'digital transformation' already indicates that data-based business models and AI will often require a considerable transformation and change process that may not be accomplished in a single step.

This stepwise procedure is a core part of the I3 – Integrated Intelligence Incubator, and it considers the fact that many data analytics solutions and intelligent algorithms will be substantially improved over the next years. Consequently, it is essential to be open to regular adaptations rather than pursuing an ideal solution in the first step. Rather, executives need to encourage agile processes with a high tolerance for failures, which will be inevitable in complex new fields like machine learning, speech synthesis, or computer vision. The 'lean startup' paradigm provides a helpful framework for proceeding in a step-by-step approach that allows for regularly considering further advances in AI and related fields.

Avoiding the pitfalls

The ten typical pitfalls can often be observed in companies from different sectors in the initial implementation of AI initiatives. In many businesses, these managerial problems emerge to some degree, but not to a hundred percent. For example, a relatively isolated implementation of several AI projects in various organizational units can be observed in many large companies, although a few of these firms have some level of central coordination. Even if these problems do not fully unfold, they are very relevant. Rather, there is a continuum from no relevance at all to a very high relevance. In light of the typical emergence of these problems, many of the pitfalls are at least somewhat relevant in the implementation of AI initiatives. Therefore, the strategies for avoiding the pitfalls and the selected methods and tools are also helpful in those companies in which a particular problem has not fully materialized. For example, the I3 – Integrated Intelligence Incubator also provides a contribution to further enhancing AI implementation in companies whose AI activities already are relatively successful.

Avoiding each of the ten pitfalls increases the chances for a successful implementation of new AI initiatives. In addition, the ten topics provide starting points for redirecting and improving ongoing AI initiatives, which have not met the initial expectations. The strategies for avoiding the pitfalls have been described at a conceptual level that enables their application in companies with diverse size and industry context. However, each of these strategies can easily be customized and specified for a company's particular situation based on a quick check-up analysis. This check-up helps to identify operational and actionable steps for each of the strategies to avoid the pitfalls. Besides these typical problems, there are additional company-specific challenges, which also need to be considered to ensure the success of AI initiatives. Here, a systematic check-up of the AI activities is also helpful because it enables executives to gain insights into the specific challenges of their company beyond the typical pitfalls.

Interestingly, many of these pitfalls refer to challenges that emerge at the beginning of AI implementation. Of course, this particular focus may derive from the fact that many firms have just started to roll out AI activities. Nonetheless, there seems to be more to this focus on challenges in the link between strategic awareness and the late-stage implementation of well-defined AI projects. In fact, many companies are fully aware of the opportunities and threats of AI. In a similar vein, they may build on their established project management organization and tools – once they have specified the particular initiatives and focus. However, it is exactly this fuzzy front end of selecting the most promising AI projects and starting their implementation, where companies experience many pitfalls. The I3 – Integrated Intelligence Incubator therefore focuses on breaking down the insights of trend analysis at a strategic level to specific operational projects that are ready for implementation according to a company's well-established project management.

The selected methods and tools only provide an initial starting point. They comprise relatively well-known tools as well as new methods that have been developed for managing digital transformation and AI or which have been substantially adapted to this particular context. For example, value chain analysis does not only refer to the traditional analysis of the current value chain in a company's industry. Rather, it includes a systematic approach to identify the expected future value chain in an intelligence-based competitive arena. This advanced value chain analysis is only one part of the I3 – Integrated Intelligence Incubator, and it helps to customize the relatively general strategies for avoiding the pitfalls with regard to the specific requirements of a single company's environmental context. The relative importance of a particular strategy for avoiding the pitfalls may differ depending on the corporate context and previous AI initiatives. However, each of the ten pitfalls and strategies usually has some relevance. Even more important, however, is an intelligent combination of multiple aspects. For example, the benefits of overcoming an excessive focus on technology and lacking business model innovation may fully unfold if companies also reduce an excessive level of perfectionism based on enabling agile experimentation across the organization.

To compile a set of specific tools, it is often helpful to collaborate with external experts, such as consulting companies, freelancers, or academics – at least for a short time. Besides fulfilling the critical role of external catalysts, such people often contribute to the identification of the most problematic pitfalls based on their external perspective and AI expertise. On this basis, they are neither biased by a company's previous AI activities nor by the existing intelligence architecture. In addition, they are not limited by a company's dominant managerial logic, which may be particularly detrimental in AI and digital innovation projects because these projects often lead to extending a company's business models. In addition, collaboration with external experts in the stages before operational execution may help to avoid failures in selecting technology providers for particular AI solutions. Many companies immediately start implementing selected AI applications rather than taking a broader portfolio perspective, including the analysis of potential synergies among multiple projects, before selecting IT providers. These companies will often not achieve their goals with AI without redirecting their initiatives at later points. Avoiding the ten most typical pitfalls is an important first step towards profiting from AI activities from the beginning of implementation.

Conclusion and outlook

The recent technological advances in diverse fields of AI already have major consequences on companies in many industries, but the largest part of the impact is yet to come. Accordingly, there is no alternative to considering the impact of AI on a company. In many sectors, it is now time to act. Other companies may still have a bit more time to react before it is too late. However, technological evolution proceeds quickly, and the growing relevance of AI cannot be ignored. Nonetheless, some executives still consider AI to be a hype that will fade in a few years. While the hype may in fact decrease a few years down the line, the strategic logic of using AI will remain. Even if the advances in AI primarily happen in the technology domain, its business impact will substantially exceed technology-related issues. In fact, the impact of AI on a company's markets, business models, and industries will have more severe consequences than the pure technological issues. Many executives have acknowledged the strategic relevance of AI and related evolutions, but the full business impact has often not been envisioned.

The further advances of AI will continue to offer opportunities and threats. Many previous discussions in the literature and press have strongly focused on the potential threats for established companies. Yes, there are competitive threats for many established business models. In a similar vein, AI applications will continue to replace a considerable number of human jobs. In this regard, the recent advances in AI are similar to previous waves of automation in earlier decades. Beyond these threats to companies and individuals, the opportunities are often overlooked to some degree. Besides threats, AI also brings numerous opportunities for companies, and efficiency gains are only one side of the coin. In the long run, the opportunities for innovation and growth may actually become more important than the optimization of the established business processes, although these efficiency benefits may often be achieved more easily. In addition, the growing implementation of AI will lead to many new jobs being generated. On this basis, it is still an open question whether the net effect of job losses and new jobs will be positive or negative in the end.

Furthermore, the recent developments in AI have already led to some emergent ethical questions. Here, a few key issues related to AI for autonomous driving have received substantial public attention. These ethical questions will become even more relevant in the future, and the importance of these topics cannot be overstated. A discussion of those highly critical questions is beyond the scope of this book. Actually, each of these key questions deserves focused attention in multiple books. For example, the potential drawbacks of AI led Google to pledge, in response to employee concerns, that it would not build weapons based on AI. This book focuses on the management implications of AI with particular emphasis on firms' possibilities to gain and sustain a competitive advantage – in the next years and decades. Thus, the book does not consider AI in terms of self-awareness systems, which describe the type of AI that is shown in movies and some future scenarios. Addressing ethical questions for such scenarios as well as for AI applications in the near future is essential for society and for the individual executive and employee even if these questions are not addressed in this book.

Rather than covering these essential ethical discussions, this book suggests an intelligence-based view of company performance, which provides a helpful framework for discussing the business implications of AI. The distinction of HI, AI, and the meta-intelligence, which all contribute to the new concept of an integrated intelligence architecture, offers new insights into the managerial impact of AI. In particular, companies need Intelligence^X – encompassing various types of AI and HI as well as the meta-intelligence. Here, the complementarity of AI and HI is as important as the renewal and recombination of a company's intelligence architecture. Overall, the intelligence-based view provides the conceptual framework for discussing the major strategic and organizational implications of AI. In this regard, a diverse set of factors needs to be considered, including business models, business ecosystems, employee attitudes, SMART leadership approaches, and many more. The diversity of these topics underscores that the impact and disruptive nature of AI goes far beyond its technological consequences.

Yes, AI will have a disruptive impact in many industries. Here, those companies that are considered the most innovative worldwide provide excellent examples. Many of these companies, such as Apple and Amazon, are well known for transforming entire industries, and they are strongly focusing on AI and related fields for many years. In this regard, the following statement of Bill Gates is remarkable: "If you invent a breakthrough in artificial intelligence, so machines can learn, that is worth 10 Microsofts."[5] This type of breakthrough will often not be feasible for a single company. Instead, ecosystems will play a growing role. Moreover, a mere focus on efficiency gains will usually not provide the basis for achieving such benefits. Most probably, many of the advanced automation procedures that are enabled by AI will become standard tools in the future, and their isolated application will not allow a competitive advantage to be gained. Instead, executives need to integrate AI with specific human expertise to outperform competitors by generating growth and innovation beyond optimization and efficiency.

In this regard, the I3 – Integrated Intelligence Incubator, which has been developed in this book, provides executives with a toolset for developing appropriate proactive and reactive strategic initiatives to enable companies to thrive amid intelligence-based future competition. AI is the dominating challenge and opportunity for firms in nearly all sectors, and it will mostly likely continue to be the key strategic topic in the next years. Therefore, executives need to act now. Rather than pursuing the separate use of AI and HI, companies should be focussing on the interfaces of AI and HI. In the long run, firms may only be able to achieve a competitive advantage if they develop and leverage Intelligence^X – comprising various types of AI and HI as well as meta-intelligence. In an intelligence-based future competitive arena, a detailed understanding of the intelligence architecture and the potential for achieving an intelligence-based competitive advantage is a critical initial step – one that calls for a proficient implementation of the selected strategies and managerial tasks. Profiting from AI is a major transformation challenge, but it is manageable and open to being addressed in a systematic way. Rather than starting with aimless activism, it is helpful to systematically examine the opportunities and threats before advancing towards implementation. I hope this book will provide some support along the exciting journey towards an intelligence-based future.

List of figures

List of tables

List of abbreviations

4S	Standard, Substitute, Superiority, Synthesis
AI	Artificial Intelligence
ATM	Automatic teller machine
Intelligence^x	Various types of artificial, human and meta-intelligence
HI	Human Intelligence
HR	Human Resources
HAIR	Human and Artificial Intelligence Resources
I3	Integrated Intelligence Incubator
IA	Intelligent-Automation
IT	Information Technology
M&A	Mergers & Acquisitions
NHI	No-Human-Interaction
OECD	Organization for Economic Co-operation and Development
R&D	Research and Development
SMART	Situational, Mutual, Analytical, Relational, and Transformational

Endnotes

Chapter 1: The competitive relevance of artificial intelligence

1 Some of the content of this discussion about the evolution of AI is also covered in my co-authored book: Ili, S., & Lichtenthaler, U. 2017. FAQ digital transformation and artificial intelligence – 101 questions & answers. Karlsruhe: Ili Consulting.

2 For further details, please see my previous article: Lichtenthaler, U. 2018. Substitute or synthesis? The interplay between human and artificial intelligence. Research-Technology Management, 61(5): 12–14.

3 Some of this discussion about technology, market, and management factors is also covered in my co-authored book: Ili, S., & Lichtenthaler, U. 2017. FAQ digital transformation and artificial intelligence – 101 questions & answers. Karlsruhe: Ili Consulting.

Chapter 2: The isolated ignorance of many established businesses

1 Please see: Christensen, C. 1997. The innovator's dilemma: When new technologies cause great firms to fail. Cambridge: Harvard Business School Press.

Chapter 3 : The strategic focus of the world's most innovative companies

1 Most parts of this chapter were adapted from my previous article, which also includes a more detailed literature overview: Lichtenthaler, U. 2018. The world's most innovative companies: A meta-ranking. Journal of Strategy and Management, 11(4): 497–511.

2 Please see: Lichtenthaler, U. 2016. Toward an innovation-based perspective on company performance. Management Decision, 54(1): 66–87.

3 For further information, please see: https://www.bcg.com/de-de/publications/collections/most-innovative-companies-2018.aspx.

4 For further information, please see: https://www.forbes.com/innovative-companies/list/#tab:rank.

5 For further information, please see: https://www.fastcompany.com/most-innovative-companies/2018.

6 For further information, please see: https://www.usatoday.com/story/money/business/2018/01/12/worlds-50-most-innovative-companies/1023095001/ and https://247wallst.com/special-report/2018/01/10/the-worlds-50-most-innovative-companies/2/.

7 For further information, please see: https://www.technologyreview.com/lists/companies/2017/.

8 Please see the description of ranking methods earlier in this chapter for further details.

9 This table was first published in my article: Lichtenthaler, U. 2018. The world's most innovative companies: A meta-ranking. Journal of Strategy and Management, 11(4): 497–511.

Chapter 4: An intelligence-based view of company performance

1 Most parts of this chapter were adapted from my previous article, which also includes a more detailed literature overview: Lichtenthaler, U. 2019. An intelligence-based view of company performance: Profiting from artificial intelligence. Journal of Innovation Management, 7(1): 15–28.

2 Please see: Bain, J.S. 1959. Industrial organization. New York: Wiley; Porter, M.E. 2008. The five competitive forces that shape strategy. Harvard Business Review, 86: 79–93.

3 Please see: Barney, J. 1991. Firm resources and sustained competitive advantage. Journal of Management, 17: 99–120; Lado, A.A., Boyd, N.G., Wright, P., & Kroll, M. 2006. Paradox and theorizing within the resource-based view. Academy of Management Review, 31: 115–131; Lambe, C.J., Spekman, R.E., & Hunt, S.D. 2002. Alliance competence, resources, and alliance success: Conceptualization, measurement, and initial test. Journal of the Academy of Marketing Science, 30: 141–158.

4 Please see: Teece, D.J. 2007. Explicating dynamic capabilities: The nature and microfoundations of (sustainable) enterprise performance. Strategic Management Journal, 28: 1319–1350; Lichtenthaler, U. 2016. Toward an innovation-based perspective on company performance. Management Decision, 54(1): 66–87.

5 Please see: Grant, R.M. 1996. Toward a knowledge-based theory of the firm. Strategic Management Journal, 17, Winter Special Issue: 109–122; Nonaka, I. 1994. A dynamic theory of organizational knowledge creation. Organization Science, 5: 14–37.

6 Please see: Gardner, H. 1983. Frames of mind: The theory of multiple intelligences. New York: Basic Books. For a more detailed literature overview, please also see my previous article: Lichtenthaler, U. 2019. An intelligence-based view of company performance: Profiting from artificial intelligence. Journal of Innovation Management, 7(1): 15–28.

7 Please see: Mueller, J. P., & Massaron, L. 2018. Artificial intelligence for dummies. Hoboken: Wiley, p. 9ff.

8 Please see: Mueller, J. P., & Massaron, L. 2018. Artificial intelligence for dummies. Hoboken: Wiley, p. 14.

9 The explanations of these different types of AI are based on multiple introductory books as well as some basic knowledge from encyclopedias. A more detailed literature review is provided in my previous article, which provides the basis for this chapter: Lichtenthaler, U. 2019. An intelligence-based view of company performance: Profiting from artificial intelligence. Journal of Innovation Management, 7(1): 15–28.

10 This figure was first published in my following article: Lichtenthaler, U. 2019. An intelligence-based view of company performance: Profiting from artificial intelligence. Journal of Innovation Management, 7(1): 15–28.

Chapter 5: Combining and complementing human and artificial intelligence

1 Many parts of this chapter have been adapted from my previous article, which also includes a more detailed literature overview: Lichtenthaler, U. 2018. Substitute or synthesis? The interplay between human and artificial intelligence. Research-Technology Management, 61(5): 12–14.

2 Please see: Winick, E. 2018. Every study we could find on what automation will do to jobs, in one chart. MIT Technology Review, 01/25/2018.

3 This figure was first published in my following article: Lichtenthaler, U. 2018. Substitute or synthesis? The interplay between human and artificial intelligence. Research-Technology Management, 61(5): 12–14.

4 Please see: Plastino, E., & Purdy, M. 2018. Game changing value from artificial intelligence: Eight strategies. Strategy & Leadership, 46: 16–22; Wilson, H. J., Daugherty, P., & Bianzino, N. 2017. The jobs that artificial intelligence will create. MIT Sloan Management Review, 58(4): 14–16.

5 Please see: Rometty, G. 2016. Digital today, cognitive tomorrow. MIT Sloan Management Review, 58(1): 168–171.

6 Please see: Plastino, E., & Purdy, M. 2018. Game changing value from artificial intelligence: Eight strategies. Strategy & Leadership, 46: 16–22.

7 Please see: Sierhuis, M., Bradshaw, J.M., Acquisti, A., Van Hoof, R., Jeffers, R., & Uszok, A. 2003. Human-agent teamwork and adjustable autonomy in practice. Proceedings of the seventh international symposium on artificial intelligence, robotics and automation in space (I-SAIRAS); Daugherty, P.R., & Wilson, H.J. 2018. Human + machine: Reimagining work in the age of AI. Boston: Harvard Business Review Press.

8 For a more detailed discussion, please see: Davenport, T.H., & Dreyer, K.J. 2018. AI will change radiology, but it won't replace radiologists. Harvard Business Review Digital Articles, 03/27/2018: 1–3; Davenport, T.H., & Ronanki, R. 2018. Artificial intelligence for the real world. Harvard Business Review, 96: 108–116.

9 Please see: Joseph, J., & Ocasio, W. 2012. Architecture, attention, and adaptation in the multibusiness firm: General Electric from 1951 to 2001. Strategic Management Journal, 33: 633–660.

10 Please see: Woyke, E. 2017. General Electric builds an AI workforce. MIT Technology Review, Online: 1–3.

11 Please see: Wilson, H.J., & Daugherty, P.R. 2018. Collaborative intelligence: Humans and AI are joining forces. Harvard Business Review, 96(4): 114–123.

12 Please see: Wilson, H.J., & Daugherty, P.R. 2018. Collaborative intelligence: Humans and AI are joining forces. Harvard Business Review, 96(4): 114–123.

13 Please see: Wilson, H.J., & Daugherty, P.R. 2018. Collaborative intelligence: Humans and AI are joining forces. Harvard Business Review, 96(4): 114–123.

14 Please see: Wilson, H.J., & Daugherty, P.R. 2018. Collaborative intelligence: Humans and AI are joining forces. Harvard Business Review, 96(4): 114–123.

15 Please see: Wilson, H.J., & Daugherty, P.R. 2018. Collaborative intelligence: Humans and AI are joining forces. Harvard Business Review, 96(4): 114–123.

Chapter 6: Renewing and recombining human and artificial intelligence

1 Many parts of this chapter have been adapted from my previous article, which also includes a more detailed literature overview: Lichtenthaler, U. 2019. Beyond artificial intelligence: Why companies need to go the extra step. Journal of Business Strategy.

2 Please see: Porter, M.E., & Heppelmann, J.E. 2015. How smart, connected products are transforming companies. Harvard Business Review, 93: 96–114.

3 Please see: Lichtenthaler, U. 2016. Toward an innovation-based perspective on company performance. Management Decision, 54(1): 66–87.

4 This figure was first published in my following article: Lichtenthaler, U. 2019. Beyond artificial intelligence: Why companies need to go the extra step. Journal of Business Strategy.

5 Please see: Galunic, D. C., & Eisenhardt, K. M. 2001. Architectural innovation and modular corporate forms. Academy of Management Journal, 44: 1229–1249; Plastino, E., & Purdy, M. 2018. Game changing value from artificial intelligence: Eight strategies. Strategy & Leadership, 46: 16–22.

6 Please see: Henderson, R., & Clark, K. 1990. Architectural innovation: The reconfiguration of existing product technologies and the failure of established firms. Administrative Science Quarterly, 35: 9–31.

Chapter 7: Business innovation and evolutionary fitness

1 Please see: Prahalad, C. K., & Bettis, R. A. 1986. The dominant logic: A new linkage between diversity and performance. Strategic Management Journal, 7: 485–501.

2 Please see: Porter, M. E., & Heppelmann, J. E. 2014. How smart, connected products are transforming competition. Harvard Business Review, 92: 64–88; Ili Consulting. 2016. Digital or dead: The digital innovation compass – Expert study. Karlsruhe: Ili Consulting; Plastino, E., & Purdy, M. 2018. Game changing value from artificial intelligence: Eight strategies. Strategy & Leadership, 46: 16–22; Ili, S., & Lichtenthaler, U. 2017. FAQ digital transformation and artificial intelligence – 101 questions & answers. Karlsruhe: Ili Consulting.

3 Please see: Ili Consulting. 2016. Digital or dead: The digital innovation compass – Expert study. Karlsruhe: Ili Consulting.

4 Please see: Ili Consulting. 2016. Digital or dead: The digital innovation compass – Expert study. Karlsruhe: Ili Consulting.

5 Ili Consulting. 2016. Digital or dead: The digital innovation compass – Expert study. Karlsruhe: Ili Consulting.

6 Please see: Ili Consulting. 2016. Digital or dead: The digital innovation compass – Expert study. Karlsruhe: Ili Consulting.

7 Please see: Porter, M. E., & Heppelmann, J. E. 2014. How smart, connected products are transforming competition. Harvard Business Review, 92: 64–88; Ili Consulting. 2016. Digital or dead: The digital innovation compass – Expert study. Karlsruhe: Ili Consulting; Ili, S., & Lichtenthaler, U. 2017. FAQ digital transformation and artificial intelligence – 101 questions & answers. Karlsruhe: Ili Consulting; Lichtenthaler, U. 2018. Substitute or synthesis? The interplay between human and artificial intelligence. Research-Technology Management, 61(5): 12–14.

8 Please see: Zahra, S. A., & George, G. 2002. Absorptive capacity: A review, reconceptualization, and extension. Academy of Management Review, 27: 185–203.

9 This section has been adapted from my previous article, which also includes a more detailed literature overview: Lichtenthaler, U. 2016. Toward an innovation based perspective on company performance. Management Decision, 54(1): 66–87.

10 Please see: Ahuja, G., Lampert, C. M., & Tandon, V. 2008. Moving beyond Schumpeter: Management research on the determinants of technological innovation. The Academy of Management Annals, 2: 1–98; Knott, A. M. 2008. R&D/returns causality: Absorptive capacity or organizational IQ. Management Science, 54: 2054–2067.

11 Please see: Helfat, C. E., Finkelstein, S., Mitchell, W., Peteraf, M. A., Singh, H., Teece, D. J., & Winter, S. G. 2007. Dynamic capabilities: Understanding strategic chance in organizations. Oxford: Blackwell Publishing.

12 Please see: Helfat, C. E., Finkelstein, S., Mitchell, W., Peteraf, M. A., Singh, H., Teece, D. J., & Winter, S. G. 2007. Dynamic capabilities: Understanding strategic chance in organizations. Oxford: Blackwell Publishing.

13 Please see: Zahra, S. A., Sapienza, H. J., & Davidsson, P. 2006. Entrepreneurship and dynamic capabilities: A review, model and research agenda. Journal of Management Studies, 43: 917–955.

14 This table and some arguments in this section were first published in similar form in my following article: Lichtenthaler, U. 2019. Intelligenz hoch drei. Next Industry, 1: 32–35.

Chapter 8: Core competencies and competitive advantage

1 Please see: Kim, W. C., & Mauborgne, R. 2014. Blue ocean strategy: How to create uncontested market space and make the competition irrelevant. Boston: Harvard Business Review Press.

2 Many paragraphs in this section were adapted from my previous article, which also includes a more detailed literature overview: Lichtenthaler, U. 2016. Toward an innovation-based perspective on company performance. Management Decision, 54(1): 66–87.

3 Please see: Dierickx, I., & Cool, K. 1989. Asset stock accumulation and sustainability of competitive advantage. Management Science, 35: 1504–1511.

4 Please see: Lin, L. 2011. Licensing strategies in the presence of patent thickets. Journal of Product Innovation Management, 28: 698–725.

5 Please see: Dierickx, I., & Cool, K. 1989. Asset stock accumulation and sustainability of competitive advantage. Management Science, 35: 1504–1511.

6 Please see: Dierickx, I., & Cool, K. 1989. Asset stock accumulation and sustainability of competitive advantage. Management Science, 35: 1504–1511.

7 Please see: Dierickx, I., & Cool, K. 1989. Asset stock accumulation and sustainability of competitive advantage. Management Science, 35: 1504–1511.

8 Many paragraphs in this section have been adapted from my previous article, which also includes a more detailed literature overview: Lichtenthaler, U. 2019. Intelligenz hoch drei. Next Industry, 1: 32–35.

Chapter 9: Value creation and value capture

1 Please see: Bettis, R. A., & Prahalad, C. K. 1995. The dominant logic: Retrospective and extension. Strategic Management Journal, 16: 5–14; Narayanan, V. K., Zane, L. J., & Kemmerer, B. 2011. The cognitive perspective in strategy: An integrative review. Journal of Management, 37: 305–351.

2 Please see: Bettis, R. A., & Prahalad, C. K. 1995. The dominant logic: Retrospective and extension. Strategic Management Journal, 16: 5–14.

3 Please see: Ili Consulting. 2016. Digital or dead: The digital innovation compass – Expert study. Karlsruhe: Ili Consulting.

4 Please see: Osterwalder, A., & Pigneur, Y. 2010. Business model generation: A handbook for visionaries, game changers, and challengers. Hoboken: John Wiley & Sons.

5 Please see: Ili, S., & Lichtenthaler, U. 2017. FAQ digital transformation and artificial intelligence – 101 questions & answers. Karlsruhe: Ili Consulting.

Chapter 10: Internal organization and external ecosystems

1 This chapter has been adapted from my previous article, which also includes a more detailed literature overview: Lichtenthaler, U. 2016. Toward an innovation-based perspective on company performance. Management Decision, 54(1): 66–87.

2 Please see: Zenger, T. R., Felin, T., & Bigelow, L. 2011. Theories of the firm-market boundary. The Academy of Management Annals, 5: 89–133.

3 Please see: Arrow, K. 1971. Essays in the theory of risk bearing. Chicago: Markham.

4 Please see: Zenger, T. R., Felin, T., & Bigelow, L. 2011. Theories of the firm-market boundary. The Academy of Management Annals, 5: 89–133.

5 Please see: Pisano, G., & Teece, D. J. 2007. How to capture value from innovation: Shaping intellectual property and industry structure. California Management Review, 50: 278–296.

6 Please see: Santos, F. M., & Eisenhardt, K. M. 2005. Organizational boundaries and theories of organization. Organization Science, 16: 491–508.

7 The content of this figure is partly adapted from my previous article: Lichtenthaler, U. 2016. Toward an innovation-based perspective on company performance. Management Decision, 54(1): 66–87.

8 Please see: Cohen, W. M., & Levinthal, D. A. 1990. Absorptive capacity: A new perspective on learning and innovation. Administrative Science Quarterly, 35: 128–152.

9 Please see: Lichtenthaler, U., & Lichtenthaler, E. 2010. Technology transfer across organizational boundaries: Absorptive capacity and desorptive capacity. California Management Review, 53: 154–170.

Chapter 11: The No-Human-Interaction paradox

1 This chapter was adapted from my previous article, which also includes a more detailed literature overview: Lichtenthaler, U. 2019. Extremes of acceptance: Employee attitudes toward artificial intelligence. Journal of Business Strategy.

2 Please see: Davis, F. D. 1989. Perceived usefulness, perceived ease of use, and user acceptance of information technology. MIS Quarterly, 13(3): 319–340.

3 Please see: Katz, R., & Allen, T. J. 1982. Investigating the Not-Invented-Here (NIH) – syndrome: A look at performance, tenure and communication patterns of 50 R&D project groups. R&D Management, 12: 7–19; Lichtenthaler, U., & Ernst, H. 2006. Attitudes to externally organising knowledge management tasks: A review, reconsideration and extension of the NIH syndrome. R&D Management, 36: 367–386.

4 Laden, K. 1996. 'Not invented there,' or, the other person's dessert always looks better! Research Technology Management, 39: 10–12. For a description of Buy-In attitudes, please see Lichtenthaler, U., & Ernst, H. 2006. Attitudes to externally organising knowledge management tasks: a review, reconsideration and extension of the NIH syndrome. R&D Management, 36: 367–386.

5 This table was first published in my following article: Lichtenthaler, U. 2019. Extremes of acceptance: Employee attitudes toward artificial intelligence. Journal of Business Strategy.

6 This figure was first published in my following article: Lichtenthaler, U. 2019. Extremes of acceptance: Employee attitudes toward artificial intelligence. Journal of Business Strategy.

7 Please see: Davis, F. D. 1989. Perceived usefulness, perceived ease of use, and user acceptance of information technology. MIS Quarterly, 13(3): 319–340.

Chapter 12: The SMART leadership framework

1 Many parts of this chapter are based on my previous article, which also includes a more detailed literature overview: Lichtenthaler, U. 2016. Six principles for shared management: A framework for the integrated economy. Journal of Business Strategy, 37: 3–11.

2 Please see: Birkinshaw, J., Hamel, G., & Mol, M. J. 2008. Management innovation. Academy of Management Review, 33: 825–845.

3 This figure was adapted from my previous article: Lichtenthaler, U. 2016. Six principles for shared management: A framework for the integrated economy. Journal of Business Strategy, 37: 3–11.

4 Please see: Hersey, P., & Blanchard, K. H. 1969. Management of organizational behavior – Utilizing human resources. Englewood Cliffs: Prentice Hall.

5　Please see: Amit, R., & Zott, C. 2012. Creating value through business model innovation. MIT Sloan Management Review, 53: 41–49.

6　Please see: Iyer, B., & Davenport, T. H. 2008. Reverse engineering Google's innovation machine. Harvard Business Review, 86: 58–68.

7　Please see: Hunt, J. G. 1999. Transformational/charismatic leadership's transformation of the field: An historical essay. The Leadership Quarterly, 10: 129–144.

8　Some of the content of this table was first published in my following article, which also includes a more detailed literature overview: Lichtenthaler, U. 2016. Six principles for shared management: A framework for the integrated economy. Journal of Business Strategy, 37: 3–11.

Chapter 13: Corporate initiatives and moving from HR to HAIR

1　This section was adapted from my previous article, which also includes a more detailed literature overview: Lichtenthaler, U. 2019. Digitale Innovationen zum Erfolg führen: Portfoliomanagement als zentrale Herausforderung. Zeitschrift Führung + Organisation.

2　This figure was first published in my following article: Lichtenthaler, U. 2019. Digitale Innovationen zum Erfolg führen: Portfoliomanagement als zentrale Herausforderung. Zeitschrift Führung + Organisation.

3　Please see: Agrawal, A., Gans, J., & Goldfarb, A. 2018. Prediction machines: The simple economics of artificial intelligence. Boston: Harvard Business Review Press.

4　The term 'HAIR' was proposed in the following article: Plastino, E., & Purdy, M. 2018. Game changing value from artificial intelligence: Eight strategies. Strategy & Leadership, 46: 16–22.

5　Please see: Plastino, E., & Purdy, M. 2018. Game changing value from artificial intelligence: Eight strategies. Strategy & Leadership, 46: 16–22.

6　Please see: Plastino, E., & Purdy, M. 2018. Game changing value from artificial intelligence: Eight strategies. Strategy & Leadership, 46: 16–22.

Chapter 14: The I3 – Integrated Intelligence Incubator

1　The analysis of value chain activities and stakeholders in a firm's environment is a typical approach in strategic management. Please see, for example, Rothaermel, F. T. Strategic management. New York: McGraw-Hill, 2018. It has also been used in the context of digital transformation. In this regard, please see, for example, Ili Consulting. 2017. Buildings and beyond – Expert study. Karlsruhe: Ili Consulting as well as my article at https://www.absatzwirtschaft.de/digitale-transformation-und-kuenstliche-intelligenz-neue-chancen-fuer-das-marketing-138323/. The company canvas in this book builds on this established logic of analyzing value chain activities and stakeholders in the extant literature.

2 Please see: Osterwalder, A., & Pigneur, Y. 2010. Business model generation: A handbook for visionaries, game changers, and challengers. Hoboken: John Wiley & Sons.

3 Please see: Osterwalder, A., & Pigneur, Y. 2010. Business model generation: A handbook for visionaries, game changers, and challengers. Hoboken: John Wiley & Sons.

4 Please see: Osterwalder, A., & Pigneur, Y. 2010. Business model generation: A handbook for visionaries, game changers, and challengers. Hoboken: John Wiley & Sons.

5 Please see: Osterwalder, A., & Pigneur, Y. 2010. Business model generation: A handbook for visionaries, game changers, and challengers. Hoboken: John Wiley & Sons.

6 Please see: Ries, E. 2011. The lean startup: How today's entrepreneurs use continuous innovation to create radically successful businesses. New York: Crown Business.

Chapter 15: Avoiding typical pitfalls in execution

1 Some of the content of the following paragraphs was first published in my following articles, which also include a more detailed literature overview: Lichtenthaler, U. 2018. Künstliche Intelligenz: Wie Führungskräfte fünf strategische Fehler vermeiden. Ideen- und Innovationsmanagement 2018 (3): 76–80. Lichtenthaler, U. 2019. Künstliche Intelligenz erfolgreich nutzen: Fünf Herausforderungen. OrganisationsEntwicklung 2019(1): 108.

2 Some of the content of this table was first published in my article: Lichtenthaler, U. 2018. Künstliche Intelligenz: Wie Führungskräfte fünf strategische Fehler vermeiden. Ideen- und Innovationsmanagement 2018 (3): 76–80.

3 Please see: Christensen, C. M., Anthony, S. D., Berstell, G., Nitterhouse, D., 2007. Finding the right job for your product. MIT Sloan Management Review 48, 38–47.

4 Please see: Kim, W. C., & Mauborgne, R. 2014. Blue ocean strategy: How to create uncontested market space and make the competition irrelevant. Boston: Harvard Business Review Press.

5 Please see: https://www.nytimes.com/2004/03/01/business/microsoft-amid-dwindling-interest-talks-up-computing-as-a-career.html.

Index